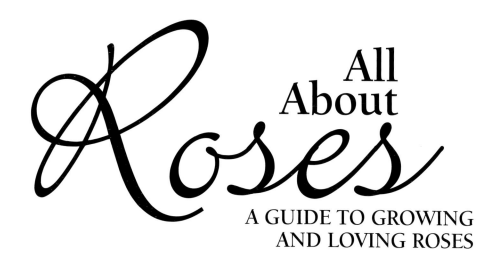

All About Roses

A GUIDE TO GROWING AND LOVING ROSES

This book is dedicated to my grandson Logan, who shared the first five years of his life with me at the rose nursery. He taught me to walk at a child's pace to truly enjoy all the incredible natural beauty within a rose garden.
Thank you Logan.

Love, Oma.

First published in 2014 by Reed New Holland Publishers Pty Ltd
London • Sydney • Auckland

The Chandlery, Unit 114, 50 Westminster Bridge Road, London SE1 7QY, United Kingdom
1/66 Gibbes Street, Chatswood, NSW 2067, Australia
218 Lake Road, Northcote, Auckland, New Zealand

www.newhollandpublishers.com

Copyright © 2014 New Holland Publishers Pty Ltd
Copyright © 2014 in text: Diana Sargeant
Copyright © 2014 in images: Diana Sargeant and Katrina Ferguson (inVision Photography)

A record of this book is held at the British Library and the National Library of Australia.

ISBN 978 1 92151 732 7

Managing Director: Fiona Schultz
Publisher: Linda Williams
Project Editor: Simon Papps
Designer: Caryanne Cleevely
Production Director: Olga Dementiev
Printer: Toppan Leefung Printing Ltd

10 9 8 7 6 5 4 3 2 1

Keep up with New Holland Publishers on Facebook
www.facebook.com/NewHollandPublishers

All About Roses

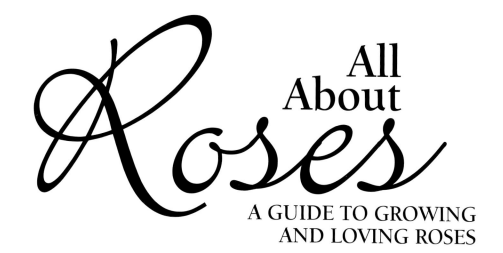

A GUIDE TO GROWING AND LOVING ROSES

Diana Sargeant

Contents

Introduction

Growing roses has been my 'job' for the past 30 years and many people have asked me to swap my office for theirs. That will never happen.

I first fell in love with roses when I fell in love with my husband Graham and no, he never promised me a rose garden, but I'm still glad I married him. Roses have given us such a depth of quality in our lives, a great understanding of the forces of nature and the opportunity to share with such beautiful people around the world who could not possibly imagine a garden without roses.

Our honeymoon in 1986 was spent at the International Rose Convention in Sydney where Graham won the Miniature Rose Championship which led to the breeder of one of his championship roses to ask us to propagate and promote that rose, 'Tracey Wickham'. Graham was working full time but I was a home mum and more than ready to take up such a challenge.

Within months we purchased the land next to our home, created rose gardens on all the wide nature strips and the inside boundaries, encroached into our neighbours' yards and registered a business called 'Silkie Gardens Rose Nursery'. In 1989 I was selected to participate in a Rotary Group Study Exchange to Texas, USA, where I was dubbed 'The Rose Lady,' and that experience changed the course of my life.

While committed to staying at home to care for the family, which was my priority, the rose nursery expanded rapidly and very soon Graham resigned from his job to join me in the business. I started presenting on a radio talkback gardening program, was guest speaker at meetings to promote growing roses for a healthy lifestyle and started to write my newsletter *Rose Rambler*.

In 1996 we renovated our delightful cottage to create the Rose Café, and after 15 years of working six days a week with the café and nursery, we sold the Kilmore site, relocated the rose business and now operate as rosesalesonline.com.au and Silkies Rose Farm at Clonbinane.

Once more I can indulge my passion for roses and plant rose gardens to my heart's content while offering rose lovers a beautiful destination to share and talk about all things roses. By being up close and personal with roses during the past 30 years of my life I have revelled in their magnificent qualities and know that, through the knowledge I am sharing in these pages, you too will become passionate about roses. Listen as the roses speak to you and take their energy to enrich your life as I have done and will continue to do.

I wish you happiness in your rose garden.

Diana

Part 1: About Roses

1.1 Rose Classification

Around the world there are different systems for classifying roses. The most simple is that used by the American Rose Society (ARS), which sets the roses into three groups: Species Roses, Heritage Roses and Modern Roses.

Species Roses

In this class are all the native roses of the world including their natural crosses. Most of the roses in this class tend to have single blooms, flower just once a year on mostly large shrubs and are very hardy in their native climates.

All roses are ultimately descended from Species Roses and it makes a fascinating challenge to do a 'family tree' from a rose in your own garden. You will be amazed at which roses were used along the way in the creation of your modern cultivar.

The rose I selected to do a 'family tree' was the most beautiful 'Queen Adelaide' and her progeny was extremely fascinating and truly interesting to study. Did the rose breeder picture her as he was busy selecting the parents for cross-pollinating? Was he surprised when such a beauty emerged?

A most comprehensive publication to help you research roses is *Modern Roses 12*. You will find the registered name of the rose, its class, colour, year of release and the name of the breeder. Next, it gives you the colour, size and shape of the flower with an indication of the depth of fragrance and type of foliage. For some varieties the thorns are mentioned as well as the size of the bush.

Sometimes the parents are listed, which is the real fun part. Who introduced the rose and the year of introduction are also indicated, along with any awards that the rose might have achieved in Rose Trial Gardens around the world.

Modern Roses 12 is a huge encyclopaedia of officially registered roses. This current edition is the most recent update in a series that dates back to 1930 and is published by the American Rose Society (ARS).

Where space permits, growing at least one true Species Rose in your garden is to grow a tribute to the history of the rose. It acknowledges the contribution that rose breeders

around the world, through their persistence, perseverance and dedication, have given us through the most beautiful modern roses which we cherish in our rose gardens today.

Rose breeders are still producing some fascinating new Modern Roses, which are directly linked to Species Roses. A series of roses is being developed from crosses of *Hulthemia persica (Rosa persica* or *R. berberidifolia)*, which was introduced in Iran in 1788. These new roses are extremely hardy, very highly fragrant and excitingly different.

Heritage Roses

In this class are all the roses that were introduced prior to 1867 and include the following, together with many thousands more:

  Bourbons

  Noisettes

  Teas

  Hybrid Spinosissimas

Previous spread: Mixed bunch of blending pinks

Top left: Queen Adelaide

Top right: Eyes for You, developed from Hulthemia persica

Top left: Stanwell Perpetual (Hybrid Spinosissima)
Bottom left: Zepherine Drouin (Bourbon)

Top right: Lamarque (Noisette)
Bottom right: Mrs B R Cant (Tea)

Heritage Roses are worthy of space in your garden. Many are repeat-flowering and have very interesting qualities. They have magnificent foliage variables and some produce the most amazing hips. A lot of varieties in this class of roses are extremely hardy, which is testament to why they are still widely grown although mostly only available at specialist rose nurseries.

If you are interested in Heritage Roses, contact the Heritage Rose Society in your region. Heritage Rose enthusiasts are vital for advancing the preservation, cultivation, distribution and study of old garden roses.

Modern Roses

This is a huge class of roses which is broken down into five distinct groups:
>Hybrid Teas and Grandifloras
>Polyanthas
>Floribundas/Cluster-flowered
>Climbers and Ramblers
>Miniatures and Patios

Bottom left: Just Joey (Hybrid Tea)   *Bottom right: Albertine (Rambler)*

Standard and Weeping Roses (sometimes referred to as 'Tree Roses') are not a class of rose in themselves because any rose can be budded to a length of rose understock to produce a standard or weeping rose effect.

David Austin's English Roses are not a separate class, and breeders who are creating very distinct types of roses like Delbard's 'Painter's Collection', Kordes's 'Rigo Rosen' and many others, are all listed in the Modern Shrubs group.

The Modern Roses class is very diverse in that every group contains every shaped rose, and therefore it is not easy for the home gardener to define which class a particular rose belongs to. Does it really matter anyway?

Every rose variety has moments in its development where it might seem to belong to one class in the morning yet appear so different by lunch time and again by dinner time. Take a look at the photos opposite of the same Charles de Gaulle rose taken during the changing phases. Charles de Gaulle is registered as a Hybrid Tea rose and we would expect,

by definition, that it would have long, single stems of classically shaped Hybrid Tea blooms. In the photo you can see the cluster of buds, which will burst forth after the original centre flower is finished – this really fits the classification of a Floribunda/Cluster-flowered rose. All the parents listed in the creation of Charles de Gaulle are Hybrid Tea roses. The flower is large with at least 60 petals, it opens slowly and has a glorious fragrance, all of which are the true traits of a classical Hybrid Tea rose.

The magnificent Dainty Bess is classified as a Hybrid Tea yet it is a single five-petal bloom – both of its parents are Hybrid Teas.

Classed Floribunda, Apricot Nectar has all the outward appearance of being a Hybrid

Bottom right: Satchmo (Floribunda)

Top left: Gra's Blue (Miniature)
Bottom left: Lions Rose (Modern Shrub)

Top & Bottom right: Charles De Gaulle
(Hybrid Tea) in different stages of bloom

Tea because of the classical-shaped blooms and the size of the bush, but there are always massive clusters of flowers as we would expect from a Floribunda. Explore the breeding line and not too far back there is the Hybrid Tea, Crimson Glory, which is the most likely factor for the Hybrid Tea qualities. All of Apricot Nectar's other parents are Floribundas.

When it all boils down, the pleasure of growing a rose is all in the performance of the plant in your garden and the enormous reward you attain from growing it well and enjoying the beautiful flowers it produces.

It does matter, however, when you see a picture of a rose and you love everything you see. You know you need to grow that rose in your garden. You must have it. You go to great lengths to acquire it but then it turns out that the bush is difficult to manage because it has diseased foliage, and it may only ever produce one or two pretty flowers in a season but otherwise sulks. Your disappointment is immense and rightly so.

You must take care when selecting roses from picture catalogues because a picture might not be a true indicator of the exact size of the bloom or the growth habit of the bush, and it definitely cannot let you smell the fragrance.

Renae (see the two images on the right of this spread) produces an amazing little flower which turns itself into the most magnificent climbing rose with clusters of up to 30 flowers on each branch. It has no thorns, extremely lush and healthy foliage and a fragrance to die for. Could you ever imagine that the blooms in the top image could develop from those in the lower photo?

More than likely not but it may, however, offer insight into how important it is to take pictures and note the names of the roses you love when you see them, then go and source them so you will grow roses which will give you enormous pleasure right from the moment you plant them. My motto is 'DO IT ONCE, DO IT RIGHT,' and this is especially important to heed when selecting and planting roses for your garden.

Tips
- *There are three main classes of roses: Species Roses, Heritage Roses and Modern Roses.*
- *Join a Rose Group in your area to learn more about roses.*
- *When selecting and planting roses: DO IT ONCE, DO IT RIGHT.*

Top right: Dainty Bess (Hybrid Tea)
Bottom right: Apricot Nectar (Floribunda)

Top left & Bottom left: blooms of Renae open to
form magnificent clusters

1.2 Rose Colours and Meanings

Roses come in the most amazing array of colours and the American Rose Society (ARS), which is the custodian of the rose registration process, has implemented the following classification scheme which divides the spectrum of rose colours into 18 distinct colour classes.

This classification may assist you when deciding which roses to select from lists and catalogues where these codes are used:

ab	apricot, apricot blend
dp	deep pink
dr	dark red
dy	deep yellow
lp	light pink
ly	light yellow
m	mauve, mauve blend
mp	medium pink
mr	medium red
my	medium yellow
ob	orange, orange blend
op	orange pink, orange pink blend
or	orange red, orange red blend
pb	pink blend
r	russet
rb	red blend
w	white, near white, white blend
yb	yellow blend

It is universally accepted that a red rose is the symbol of love and fidelity and giving red roses continues to be a very popular way to say "I love you."

Opposite page: Loving Memory

Top left: In Appreciation
Bottom left: Memoire

Top right: Casanova
Bottom right: Paradise

The bright, sunny colour of yellow roses evokes a feeling of warmth and happiness. Those warm feelings associated with a yellow rose are akin to sharing with a true friend. As such, the yellow rose is a symbol for friendship.

A pink rose can be given as an expression of admiration, and it is a symbol of grace and elegance. Pink roses also convey appreciation and joyfulness, which just so happen to be reflected in the names of two beautiful pink roses

White roses represent innocence and purity, honour and reverence, which is why brides traditionally carry white roses. An arrangement of white roses and red roses is often used for remembrance.

Orange roses are the embodiment of desire and enthusiasm and they symbolize passion, excitement and energy.

Mauve roses are a perfect symbol of enchantment and they have captured many hearts and dreams. They are also traditionally used to express feelings of love at first sight.

Some roses are named according to their colour significance and there are many, many such aptly named roses where the colour matches the name so that when you gift a rose, there can also be a message denoted in the colour of the flower.

1.3 Different Shapes of Rose Flowers

Rose flowers come in the most extensive range of colours of almost any plant. To add to their popularity and beauty, they also come in an amazing variety of magnificent shapes that fall into five distinct categories:

Top right: Close to You

Single – usually only five petals with a magnificent display of stamens and generally associated with Species Roses/old-fashioned roses or what a lot of gardeners call 'wild roses'. Some single-petal roses are very enduring as cut flowers in the vase. They are very showy with the sheer volume of blooms.

Hybrid Tea – is the classic rose shape of a long bud with an average of 50 petals. The bloom opens slowly to eventually reveal the stamens. This continues to be the most popular rose shape for home gardeners and is the rose shape of choice in the florist industry.

Semi-double – a loose arrangement of up to 20 petals, which open and reveal the stamens. This shape is usually associated with the Floribunda or Cluster-flowered group of roses.

Rosette – masses of smaller, very pointed and ruffled petals which lie flat and have a small button-eye in the centre hiding the stamens. They are very long lasting on the bush or in a vase and are found in all classes.

Quartered, Cupped – plump round buds open into deep urns revealing a swirling mass of four sections of petals rotating around four different centres. Many old-fashioned roses, David Austins and modern shrub roses have beautiful quartered petal formations.

There is a quite distinct shaped rose bloom emerging that does not fit any of the above categories. A number of recently released roses have a very stiff waved petal form, which tends to split at the end of each petal. The flowers are very enduring, lasting more than three weeks on the bush when fully opened, and this also makes these varieties especially useful and appealing as roses for a vase.

Maybe there will be a sixth flower form that could be named 'Waved Petal' and we will see it added to registered flower shapes in the not too distant future. How delightful that we always have something to look forward to because the rose breeders of the world are enthusiastically trying to achieve 'the perfect rose'.

As I walk around my garden, and see one perfect rose after another, I am reminded constantly of the rose breeders' high levels of imagination and persistence, which are required to create such magnificence.

How ever could roses be better than they are today? Tomorrow will tell a whole new story and we who love the rose wait in anticipation of what those rose breeders might conceive.

1.4 Rose Fragrance

When one person touches something cold, then another person touches the same object, under normal circumstances both would experience a feeling of cold. However, when it comes to the fragrance of a rose, the sensory experiences of people can be highly variable. After I smell a rose where I detect a heavenly fragrance, I pick the rose in order to share the pleasure. I pass you the flower and you smell it immediately after me.

Wrap your hands around the bloom to warm the petals; the heat in your palms releases the fragrance. Take first a light sniff then a breath of fresh air. Now deeply inhale through your nostrils.

It is very possible that you detect no fragrance at all, which is very perplexing but proves that our olfactory sense is extraordinarily different, as I could never have breathed all the perfume out of the rose before you smelled it.

Left: Pope John Paul II   *Right: Perfume Passion*

If fragrance is the most important reason for you to grow and enjoy roses in your garden then you definitely should buy potted roses on a warm, sunny day while the roses are flowering and when even mildly perfumed roses are most likely to emit their fragrance.

If the first rose you sink your nose into is very highly fragrant, the next few roses you sniff may seem to have no fragrance at all. When this happens, take a few deep breaths or blow your nose and go back to smell the rose you thought had no fragrance; you will now detect a perfume because you cleared the original fragrance from your nose.

Rose fragrance is a complex blend of fruits like apple, peach, raspberry, bergamot, citrus, and more. There can be sweet floral tones of jasmine, gardenia, geranium, lavender or lilac and lots of other flowers. Fragrant spices like vanilla, cloves and cinnamon can be detected, and the intense woody smell of moss, sandalwood, myrrh and frankincense from trees. There are so many wonderful and different fragrances to enjoy.

Pop a little bit of all those plants in a blender and it comes out smelling like a rose as there is a hint of any one of those fragrances in all roses.

Every rose's perfume alters by varying degrees during the flowers' development. Some varieties are intensely fragrant on the bush but lose their heady fragrance in a vase. For other varieties the reverse happens. On a damp cold morning one might expect no fragrance in the rose blooms but there are rose varieties that wait for just such a moment to emit their most delicious perfume and then shut down during a hot sunny afternoon.

To my nose, there are some roses that **always** have intense fragrance no matter the time of day, whether the weather is hot or cold, or if the flower is on the bush or in a vase:

Pope John Paul II
Abraham Darby
Perfume Passion
Soeur Emmanuelle
Black Caviar
Saint Cecilia
Firefighter
Rhapsody-in-Blue
Gra's Blue

Top left: Rhapsody-in-Blue
Bottom left: Firefighter

Top right: Abraham Darby
Bottom right: Black Caviar

Your list of most highly fragrant roses would differ from mine simply because we all have a different sense of smell.

Rose fragrance has a mood, which changes, just as your mood alters when you smell the heady fragrance of a rose. It is, therefore, really important to take quiet moments to stop and smell the roses!

Tips
- *Every rose has a fragrance.*
- *Feeling stressed? Take time out to smell the roses.*

1. 5 What's in a Name?

All the roses we grow in our gardens today originated from about 250 species of rose which were in existence in the northern hemisphere some 30 million years ago. Today, there are about 50,000 cultivars of roses grown around the world and large rose-breeding companies on every continent produce a staggering 3 million seedling roses every year.

The seedling roses are planted in trial beds to check their worthiness for release for commercial production. This arduous process can take many years as bud wood is posted around the world and shared with other rose growers and production nurseries to see if the seedling rose performs in a variety of different environments.

There are amateur rose breeders all around the globe too – rose gardeners just like you and me who allow their curiosity get the better of them and cross one of their favourite roses with another, produce a few seedlings and see if they have a commercially viable new variety.

What this means is that every single year thousands of new varieties of roses are released around the world and it is the job of the home gardener to collect catalogues, meander through public and private rose gardens, specialist rose nurseries and garden centres trying to decide which rose variety would be better than another – a very daunting and fun pastime.

You know you're hooked on roses once you start reading rose catalogues instead of

Opposite: Soeur Emmanuelle

a novel at bedtime. To assist you with selecting what you REALLY want in a rose, the following is a broad description of the different types of roses within the Modern Roses class, together with details of the growth habits of each one.

Hybrid Tea roses

More commonly referred to as bush roses, the Hybrid Teas have a traditional upright growth habit and on average grow to a height of 1.2–1.5m (4–5ft). The bushes produce classically shaped, large flowers on long stems, which open rather slowly and are perfect for exhibiting in a vase.

Many Hybrid Tea roses are very highly fragrant, some have little or almost no fragrance and they come in a vast array and blend of colours.

Hybrid Teas can also be bi-coloured like 'Double Delight', reverse bi-coloured such as 'New Kleopatra,' or striped as in 'Tropical Sunset.'

The popularity of these magnificent roses has not waned since the first Hybrid Tea 'La France' was registered in 1867. The breeder, Guillot in France, combined the grace and elegance of a Tea rose with the vigour and hardiness of a Hybrid Perpetual rose which are both repeat flowering and thus, a whole new class of roses was born.

There is a beautiful book, *For Love of a Rose*, written by Antonia Ridge about the breeding process and family history of one of the world's most famous and favourite roses of all time, the Hybrid Tea 'Peace'. This is highly recommended reading for those wishing to attain a greater appreciation of the persistence, diligence and dedication required to breed a new rose.

Above: Double Delight

Floribunda/Cluster-flowered Roses

This group of roses produces a spray or cluster of medium-sized blooms with an open petal formation on one stem. Floribunda rose bushes are generally short, rounded bushes growing to an average height of between 75–120cm (30–48in). They are used to great effect when planted in groups of the same variety because they create a continual free-flowering mass of colour over a long flowering season.

Floribunda roses were developed by crossing Hybrid Teas with polyantha roses (*R. chinensis x R. multiflora*), the trait of this parent being that some Floribundas have fewer thorns as is the case with the most widely grown, very popular Floribunda 'Iceberg' and its sports.

Mass plantings of Floribundas are used in public parks and gardens, roadside plantings and, of course, home gardens, where they are used for great visual impact. They are very low-maintenance roses because the spent flowers can be removed with loppers or mechanical hedgers.

Top left: New Kleopatra   *Top right: Tropical Sunset*

Climbers and Ramblers

By broad definition, a rambling rose puts all its energy into growing long, branching canes and then only flowers during spring/early summer with a massive display of blooming clusters followed by rose hips in the autumn when left unpruned. Ramblers are very useful when planted where they can cover unsightly structures or screen along great lengths of fencing as they require very little maintenance and will continue to grow and grow if left unpruned.

Climbing roses flower continually throughout the flowering season. Because of their generous flowering ability, climbing roses are usually more moderate in height and width growth habit but require careful consideration when purchasing because most climbing roses produce thorny canes no less than 3m (10ft) long and they have no built-in mechanism to cling to walls or wind themselves around a support.

One of the greatest considerations when selecting which climbing rose to plant revolves around the thorns or lack of them and there are a good number of climbing roses which have few or no thorns and can be safely used in a public thoroughfare, along the driveway fence, as a wind protection screen in the vegetable garden, or even over the kids' play house.

Miniatures and Patio Roses

Ideal for growing in containers or along the edge of a garden border these delightful little plants come in every colour and shape of all the other rose classes. The only difference is that they are small in flower shape and leaf size with bush height of less than 1m (3ft) tall.

Most varieties should be trimmed constantly to encourage rapid repeat flowering. These are the roses to use if you wish to entice your children to enjoy the rose garden with you. The prickles are not ferocious and even if the children pruned the rose 'wrong' a mini rose would accept it and just get on with another round of flowering.

Opposite: Iceberg & Bonica Floribundas

Modern Shrubs

We are seeing stunningly healthy, low maintenance, free-flowering varieties of roses in the Modern Shrub class as rose breeders focus on creating roses that grow without the need for chemical spraying to sustain them.

Most Modern Shrub roses display dark green, leathery and glossy foliage which is naturally resistant to pests and diseases and makes them suitable for planting on a broad-scale in public parks and gardens because, once planted, they require very little maintenance other than regular watering and fertilizing to establish and mechanical pruning once or twice a year.

For the home gardener these roses offer tough, extremely hardy, low maintenance, disease resistant and very floriferous rose bushes with all the qualities they love about roses.

Lots of Modern Shrubs display a Hybrid Tea-style flower then open with the quartered, old-fashioned-style petal formation. Many have magnificent fragrance, which is becoming increasingly important and the reason that so many gardeners choose to

Left: Casanova showing healthy foliage

Right: Forget-me-not
Opposite page: Gra's Blue

plant roses. The breeders have noted this fact and now that the health issues of roses have been addressed through the creation of these very healthy, disease-resistant Modern Shrubs, rose fragrance is now a very high priority in their breeding programs as is evident in so many recently released varieties.

The Modern Shrubs come in a diverse range of bush size, ranging from 75–200cm (30–80in), and generally grow as wide as they are tall. Carefully read the plant labels or catalogue description, as it is important to take the size factor into account when selecting shrub roses in order to accommodate them in the allocated site.

1.6 Why Grow Roses?

When you see roses flowering in gardens all around you for months and months on end, you too will be inspired to grow roses in your garden. Make a visit to the local garden centre or rose farm and I know you will be unable to resist impulsively buying at least one rose, either for your garden or as a gift for somebody for a special occasion. There are lots of reasons to grow roses.

For Colour. Maybe you want lots of colour in your garden and Modern Roses will most certainly provide six to nine months of virtually continual flowering, filling the garden with a plethora of colour variety that is almost exclusively found only in the selection of roses available today.

The future of modern roses might include the ultimate true delphinium blue rose or roses that have polka dots. Those are two things which rose breeders haven't yet managed to breed in roses and I'm not sure I would like either.

With roses of all different heights available it is possible to create a palette of colour from fence-top height to a low rose-hedge along the border of the garden path and most definitely everywhere in between, no matter how large or small the garden space. Don't get lost in trying to sort which colour goes with what because it all works when there is a massive and random selection of colours.

For Fragrance. Fragrant roses will easily seduce you and with careful selection you can have an abundance of distinctly variable perfumes in your rose garden. There are fragrant roses in every class. Tiny miniature roses and single-petal rose blooms can be highly fragrant.

If you only want fragrant roses in your garden, purchase your roses when they are potted specimens in flower because every individual has a different sense of smell and the catalogue description of fragrance will be written by somebody who undoubtedly will have a totally different perception of rose perfume than you do.

For Relaxation. There is a huge selection of extremely healthy, disease-resistant modern shrub roses available now and when they are planted in a well-designed rose garden with an automatic watering system installed, the rose garden will be very low- maintenance and offer you a beautiful space where you can unwind and relax.

Your rose garden should be a place you are pleased to come home to; the space where you are inspired to while away some quiet moments picking a bunch of flowers to take and pop on your desk at work.

For a Challenge. Exhibiting roses can be a challenging and rewarding extension of the pleasure you will gain from growing roses in your garden.

There are Rose Societies or garden clubs in most cities and towns. They hold regular meetings along with competitive rose shows where you are able to display the magnificent roses from your garden. Imagine your pleasure and excitement when the rose you entered is awarded first prize in its class or the coveted 'Champion Rose of the Show'.

For Sharing. Having a rose garden offers you an amazing opportunity to share with people around you. If you belong to a community group in your town they will enjoy you picking bunches of roses and showing them off at local events. Take them to your favourite coffee shop and see how quickly you strike up a conversation about your gardening prowess.

Your neighbours will want to chat with you about the garden while you're out fussing with the roses and this can lead to a happy relationship just like our amazing experience during 25 years at the Rose Nursery in Kilmore.

Our neighbours Clarrie and Joyce became our most treasured friends. Clarrie retired soon after we started the nursery and needed something to keep him occupied so we planted a few roses on his side of the street. He was tending them constantly so we added more roses, and as the display gardens were developed on our side of the street he asked for more roses on his side.

Two huge trees were removed from their yard to make room for even more roses. Eventually, the whole dead-end side street became a public rose garden for nursery visitors and passers-by to enjoy. We received commendation from the local council for how the rose garden enhanced the township entrance.

Clarrie and Joyce maintained those gardens until they died in their late 80s and they always told us how the rose gardens gave them great purpose and added enormous quality to their lives.

If you only ever plant one rose, this might be a very good reason to do so:

To Shade an Area for your Pets. The hutch in our dog run enclosure was exposed to very hot sun and the dogs were unable to shelter there until the rambling rose 'Vielchenblau' established itself. During winter when the rose defoliates there is a beautifully sunny concrete apron where the dogs love to lounge around and enjoy the warm winter sun. In summer it's delightfully shaded and cooled by the lush rose foliage.

Vielchenblau smothers itself with small clusters of fragrant purple flowers

Above: Vielchenblau

for around six weeks during spring and early summer and is very attractive to bees. If the rambler is not trimmed immediately after flowering it produces masses of rose hips during autumn, when the foliage also changes colour before it falls.

Plant a Special Gift Rose you received. You had an event in your life and somebody presented you with a beautiful rose plant to celebrate the occasion. Be sure to plant it in a prominent spot in your garden where it will be most appreciated.

When we demolished the street gardens at the Kilmore nursery, Graham made a really special effort to retain three plants of my treasured highly fragrant Hybrid Tea rose 'Jardins de Bagatelle,' which now flowers magnificently just off the veranda where I sit with my morning cuppa so that I can enjoy the waft of sweet rose fragrance before the busy-ness of another day.

Left: Rose hips

Right: Jardins de Bagatelle

Fill a Sunny Space with a Potted Rose. In any garden there is usually a sunny position where it may be impossible to plant into the ground because of paving. Using an urn or decorative pot, plant a high-health, low maintenance rose to dress up the space. Make sure there is a tap close by to easily access daily watering, which is necessary for any contained rose.

'Tintern Rose' is nearly always flowering and the way it spills from the urn is very appealing. This ground-covering rose, which has a delightful fragrance, flowers continually for no less than nine months each season and retains extremely healthy foliage throughout the season.

To Welcome You Home. The perfect location for such a happy, smiling rose like 'Guy Savoy' is on a post at the driveway entrance. This continually blooming, delightfully fragrant rose greets me as I enter the driveway and it never ceases to amaze me that one rose can display such an awesome array of differently striped blooms in such abundance. It's a true 'welcome home' rose.

To Shade an Alfresco Dining Area.
Within a year of planting three 'Alberic Barbier' weeping roses on Hills Hoists (clothes lines) at the Rose Café in Kilmore, the alfresco dining area was fully shaded by roses and became a most popular area for visitors.

The rambling rose 'Alberic Barbier' has vicious hooked thorns and needed to be constantly pruned so that arching canes permitted people to walk under and through the canopy of dense, dark green, shiny foliage and continual profusion of lightly fragrant flowers.

In late autumn each year the roses had

Above: Tintern Rose
Opposite page: Guy Savoy

to be heavily pruned to allow the sunshine into the dining area, otherwise it became just too cold to sit there. By the time the sun got hot in late spring and early summer, the roses were fully foliaged and flowering again.

To Cover the Arch at your Front Entrance. This photo of a 'Dorothy Perkins' rambling rose flowering in the spring of 1958 oozes love and pride in this couple's beautiful garden in Melbourne, Australia. Dear 'Dorothy Perkins' is not grown much these days because she was a renowned 'mildew magnet' and only flowered profusely in the springtime.

To create such a magnificent sight in your garden today, I would recommend the very special rose 'Renae' because it is totally thornless, flowers in clusters over a very long season, is highly fragrant and has the most pretty mid-green shiny foliage. 'Renae' is a rose which ticks all the boxes for planting over the lichgate, pergola, archway, in an obelisk or in any location where you need to cover something ordinary and make it look stunningly beautiful with ease.

To Attract Bees into the Garden. A group of three plants of *Rosa rugosa* strategically placed close to the vegetable garden or orchard, would attract enough bees to pollinate all your vegetables and fruit trees. *Rugosa* roses have stunningly healthy foliage, which is serrated, and the plants grow at least 1.5x1.5m (5x5ft) requiring very little management once well established.

If the flowers are not dead-headed in late summer, the most incredible harvest of plump, highly nutritious rose hips can be either left on the plants for the birds to enjoy or picked and used for the family to enjoy as rose-hip jam.

Above: Arch in Melbourne Garden

To Enjoy Fragrance through an Open Window. If there is a lovely sunny location outside a frequently opened window or door, plant a highly fragrant rose like 'The Children's Rose' there to naturally freshen the house on a sunny day.

One large bush like 'The Children's Rose,' which grows to 1.5m (5ft) whether in the ground or in a large pot, will produce enough fragrance to enjoy cut flowers in a vase on the kitchen bench and leave an adequate supply of blooms on the bush outside as well. This rose produces masses of near-thornless stems of intoxicatingly fragrant flowers on a strong and very healthy bush continually throughout the flowering season.

Welcome Entrance. Every time I walk in or out of the back door, there is 'Papi Delbard' greeting me with the most gloriously petal-filled blooms of magnificent beauty. Plant this rose where you can visit it frequently, lean over and sniff the magic of its fragrance and snip a flower for a little vase in the bathroom or on your desk at work to simply brighten your day; 'Papi Delbard' and 'Abraham Darby,' which is planted very close nearby, are two gentlemen who are welcome residents in my garden.

Whatever the reason for planting one rose or a hundred roses in your garden, be sure to follow our simple, economical rose management tips and you will enjoy the queen of flowers for many, many years.

Above: Rosa rugosa 'Scabrosa' *with bees*

1.7 Gift Roses

Rose breeders are now rewarded for their efforts in producing new roses for us to enjoy. When a new rose is registered a royalty payment through Plant Breeders' Rights (PBR) is paid to the breeder for every rose sold.

If a rose is blessed with a really famous person's name it is guaranteed to be popular. A catchy name is great too, like 'Playboy,' 'First Love' or 'Happy Anniversary,' because the rose can be used as a gift for a special purpose or occasion. Many charity organisations such as the Red Cross raise significant amounts of money by having a rose named for them and this can entice gardeners to purchase the rose as a way of donating funds to that particular charity.

Left: The Children's Rose

Right: Bunch of Delbard roses

Examples of this include:

- The RSPCA is paid a royalty for every 'Best Friend' rose sold and many pets' graves are adorned with this magnificent rose.
- Children's Hospitals throughout Australia have received the royalty payment each 'The Children's Rose' is sold.
- Very appropriately the proceeds of the beautiful rose Forget-me-Not go to Alzheimer's Australia SA Inc.
- Roses make a beautiful gift. Whether it's a bunch of roses from your garden or long-stemmed specimens from the florist, rose flowers are always appreciated.

There are many roses with names that match particular occasions and it is possible to purchase a potted rose plant in flower so that when the recipient plants the rose, they have an enduring reminder of the occasion because it will continue to flower in their garden.

The following are just a few very special roses, which can be successfully grown either in the ground or in tubs on a balcony, with suitable names to match different occasions:

One Love (rb) Floribunda, dark purple-red buds open to reveal yellow stamens as the petals fade to rich cerise with glossy lime-green foliage; spicy fragrance.

Golden Celebration (yb) Austin, warm golden swirling mass of exceptionally fragrant petals in deeply cupped blooms; large shrub with dark green foliage.

Above: Playboy

Linked Hearts (lp) HT, palest pink perfectly formed blooms with incredible fragrance; extraordinary healthy glossy foliage.

My Hero (mp) Shrub, massive clear pink blooms with strong spicy fragrance; lush dark glossy foliage.

Spirit of Peace (ab) HT, creamy apricot perfectly formed blooms on long stems with exquisite fruity fragrance; tall healthy bush.

Memoire (w) HT, pure white beautifully formed large flowers with subtle tea-rose

Left: Happy Anniversary

Right: Best Friend
Opposite page: One Love

fragrance; strong dark, very healthy foliage on compact bush.

Many Happy Returns (lp) Shrub, pale pink fading to white, semi-single blooms in trusses on healthy branching shrub; produces masses of hips if unpruned.

Remember Me (or) HT, fawn centre with orange-red outer petals on classic buds; extremely healthy glossy foliage on tall upright bush.

The list goes on but I recommend you always take time to consider what type of rose you are gifting and appropriately match it to the recipient and possibly also to their garden situation.

There is a magnificent old-fashioned rambling rose called 'Wedding Day' which is appropriately named to present as a wedding day gift. For people who have a very large garden the rose would be entirely suitable, however 'Wedding Day' is most unsuitable for a couple who live in a townhouse and need to plant the rose in a container on their balcony.

Most of us won't ever forget our wedding day, but the 'Wedding Day' rose, planted in a small garden or in a pot on a balcony, will make the recipients of that gift rose wish they had never been married. 'Wedding Day' is a very thorny, hugely rampant rose which only flowers in the spring and would never, ever reach its magnificent potential in a tub on a balcony.

On the other hand, 'The Wedding Rose' is a beautiful, pure white, highly fragrant, very healthy rose, which flowers continually throughout the season and is a perfectly named rose for a wedding gift but also suitable in any garden situation or large pot.

Take care to consider the recipient's

Above: Golden Celebration

Top left: Linked Hearts

Bottom left: Spirit of Peace

Top right: Many Happy Returns

Bottom right: Wedding Day rambler

garden situation when selecting a rose gift and you will be sure to be remembered with pleasure when the gifted rose blooms year after year.

Tips
- *Breed a rose and call it anything you like.*
- *Consider all the qualities of the rose you are gifting and match it to the recipient's garden situation.*
- *Donate to your favourite charity by purchasing a rose named in their honour.*

1.8 Children in the Rose Garden

People often ask for thornless roses and when I ask "why thornless?" they talk about their children potentially being hurt by the prickles on the roses. It exasperates me because kids actually love roses – they scoot around between the potted roses in the nursery and after the first scrape against a rose, they discerningly lift their little arms up and keep on walking, stopping frequently to touch and smell the flowers and they always enjoy gathering rose petals from the ground to take home and make all sorts of creative 'things' with. Children are so attuned to nature.

A week after our daughter-in-law Justine had her baby, she insisted on coming back to work as Café Manager; Logan came too. The ensuing years were some of the happiest times at the Rose Nursery watching this little boy grow up around the roses.

Logan's entertainment and stimulation was watching rose petals flutter in the breeze and clouds moving in the sky. When he could sit up, his pram was set in the chook yard to watch the fowls scurry through the compost heap and there were times when I almost forgot that he was there until he cried for attention. He crawled through potted roses, took his first teetering steps around them and once fell head first into some roses but came away without a scratch.

Taking time to enjoy nature at his pace put a whole new perspective on how I viewed the roses. I stopped and watched ladybirds munching on aphids, looked closely at and touched frogs, grasshoppers, praying mantises and all sorts of other insects that abound

Opposite page: The Children's Rose with praying mantis

in an eco-friendly garden. I now know that skinks (lizards) can hang on to kids' fingers with their gums and you must tickle their tummies so they let go.

When other kids came to the rose nursery, Logan would take them on adventures looking for frogs and worms, he would show them how to make mud pies and, although they usually left the nursery with a bit of dirt on their clothes, the smiles on their faces were a priceless indication of the fun moments they had enjoyed in the rose garden.

Let the children free to explore all the treasures in a rose garden. Give them a bucket of water, and little containers so they can make homes for the frogs and insects they find. There might be the odd incident when they get a scratch or a bite but nature will nurture them.

Planting roses in a garden where your children are likely to play will not be an issue for them. Roses don't offer bad news, disturbing images or criticism, but rather reinforce self-esteem, encourage self-discipline and offer them magical moments to stimulate their imagination.

Hide so they cannot see you and listen to their conversations with nature and the children will teach you how to slow down and enjoy wonders you never thought possible within your rose garden.

Children quickly learn to respect that roses grow prickles and when their ball goes into the rose bushes, they'll yell out for Dad to get the ball out from under the rose bush. Dad will call Mum and she'll retrieve the ball in no time.

If you are still concerned about thorny roses around the children, here is a list of roses which I consider to be appropriately less thorny:

Gold Medal

Ekstase

Sweet Intoxication

Perfume Passion

Fabulous

Tuscan Sun

Shady Lady

Firefighter

Charles de Gaulle
Lavender Simplicity
Pope John Paul II
Dioressence
First Love
Blue for You
Playboy

There are many, many more so if you are definitely averse to growing roses with lots of prickles, you should purchase your roses while they are well-established potted specimens so that you can evaluate their thorny status before you buy them.

This page: Garden Harvest - Tomatoes and Summer Memories roses

Next spread: Moonbeam with 'Blue for You' in background

Part 2: Which Rose For My Garden?

2.9 Hedges of Roses

Whatever your specification of height and width, there is a rose variety which will create a hedge of colour to either form an internal divider in the garden or create a sense of privacy on a boundary of your property.

Depending on the variety of rose selected, a rose hedge can be an ornamental feature but might well perform as an impenetrable barrier. Very careful consideration should be given to the reason for creating a hedge of roses.

Short and Narrow Rose Hedge

There is not a single rose that could ever replace a 50x50cm (18x18in) English box hedge without an extreme amount of constant trimming which would thus reduce the flowering capacity and you may hardly ever see a rose bloom at such a restricted height and width.

However, from 75x75cm (30x30in) upwards to 120x120cm (48x48in) the following varieties of roses will suitably perform to create such a hedge:

Bonica (mp-lp)
La Sevillana (mr)
Iceberg (w)
Frau Dagmar Hastrup (lp)
Busy Bee (mp)
Lion's Rose (w)
Peach Profusion (ab)
Mary Rose (mp)
Play Boy (ob)
China Girl (my)
Hommage a Barbara (dr)
Gra's Blue (m)

Above: Hommage a Barbara

This is only a very small indication of the number of varieties in each colour range, which would most certainly suit a hedge of short to medium height and width. Densely planting the roses by spacing them from 50–75cm (20–30in) apart will ensure rapid development of a hedge and trimming maintenance could be performed with good sharp hedge-shears or mechanical hedging equipment.

Tall and Narrow Rose Hedge

To create a tall yet narrow hedge of roses, I recommend a simple support frame be built using long steel stakes with reinforcing wire mesh securely attached for permanent and durable support. If there is little or no pedestrian or vehicular traffic on either side of this hedge of roses, the quickest roses to cover the frame will be some of the very thorny rambling roses planted at 3m (10ft) apart for quick cover, or 5m (16ft) apart if you are prepared to wait a few seasons for complete coverage. A selection is as follows:

Left: Pinkie climbing   *Right: Crepuscule*

Albertine (pb)
Wedding Day (w)
New Dawn (lp)
Dublin Bay (mr)
Lamarque (w)Clg. Gold Bunny (dy)

Alternatively, the following thornless rambling rose varieties are suitable where consideration should be given to pedestrian traffic:

Veilchenblau (m)
Pinkie (mp)
Crepuscule (ab)
Mme Alfred Carriere (w)
Zepherine Drouin (dp)
Renae (lp)

If there are no specifications other than a lot of colour for a tall and narrow hedge to create a dense barrier, almost any climbing rose would suit the location.

To achieve the desired effect, most climbing roses will require some amount of effort in the first two years of establishment in order to spread and attach the climbing canes to the wall. Once covering the frame, pruning with a mechanical hedger will adequately contain the roses to a hedging effect with minimal maintenance.

NEVER WEAVE THE CANES THROUGH THE MESH, but rather attach the canes with a light jute string or other similar perishable material, because when it comes to pruning the rose hedge during the ensuing years it will be nigh impossible to extract thick climbing rose canes if they have been wound through mesh.

Short and Wide Rose Hedge

Modern shrub roses, which include the David Austin English roses and ground covering/landscape roses, fit this specification perfectly as every flower shape, every colour and every fragrance is available. I recommend thorough research so that you select exactly the type of rose you want for your hedge of roses.

Many of the roses in this class, planted at around 75cm (30in) spacing, can be pruned to fit the space of 100cm (33in) high to 120cm (48in) wide without interfering with the flowering performance. Without pruning, the hedge will easily become 120x120cm (48x48in) as the lax canes, heavy with flowers, will branch out widely as the bushes join together.

With careful selection, you could purchase a whole variety of different-coloured modern shrubs or ground-covering roses and end up with the most amazingly colourful hedge of low-maintenance, very free-flowering roses which can be maintained to a nominated hedge width and height with mechanical pruning. Some highly recommended roses are:

      Knockout (dp)
      Summer Memories (w)
      Tintern (ob)

Left: Lavender Dream hedge   *Right: Unpruned Knockout hedge*

Lavender Dream (m)
Shooting Star (yb)
Mainau Feur (r)

Tall and Wide Rose Hedge

Where space permits for a tall and wide rose hedge then look no further than amongst some of the magnificent old-fashioned roses, because this is where they come into their own. *Rugosa* roses and their hybrids, many of the Tea Roses and the Hybrid Musks, as well as many David Austin roses, are all suitable for creating a wonderfully rewarding and almost impenetrable hedge of continual flowering roses if given the space to do so. The hedge can be maintained to grow at least 1.5x1.5m (5x5ft).

Varieties within each group of these roses have individually remarkable qualities such as foliage type, production of hips and other attractive attributes.

The following roses all grow beautifully with extraordinary health and vigour, are

Left: Rosa rugosa 'Alba'   *Right: Graham Thomas*

abundantly free-flowering throughout the season and require little or no maintenance once established. This makes them exceptional where the requirement is for a tall and wide hedgerow of roses:

Rosa chinensis 'Mutabilis' (ob-rb)
Rosa rugosa 'Scabrosa' (dp)
Rosa rugosa 'Alba' (w)
Lady Hillingdon (ab)
Graham Thomas (yb)
Penelope (w)

My suggestion would be to turn your front nature strip into a bed of colourful roses to save having to mow the lawns on the weekend. Your neighbours will soon follow suit and then all the kids in the neighbourhood will be pitching in to dig, dung, water and prune the nature strips in their street. There is no doubt that this will generate a significant amount of pride in the place where you all live.

2.10 Climbers, Ramblers, Pillars and Thornless

Climbing Roses

Roses in this class can create the backbone of a beautiful rose garden. They will add height around the boundary by covering walls and fences. They will create spires of colour if given an obelisk frame to fill or they might be budded to a weeping rose understock for a central focal point in the middle of the lawn. Whatever the structure you want to cover, there is a climbing rose variety which will oblige.

Climbing roses are stunning when they've been espaliered (trained and tied onto a frame) where they can really show off their magnificent beauty. This requires time and diligent management to establish and always, if the right rose is selected to adorn a specific structure, the result will be years of awesome focal delight.

Here are a few of the most highly recommended climbing roses in each colour category:

Apricot 'Crepuscule' – Massive clusters of blooms continually throughout the season, lush healthy foliage and very few thorns.

Apricot-pink 'Abraham Darby' – One of the most beautiful, charming and fragrant David Austin roses that flowers throughout the season.

Blush-white 'Sea Foam' – Amazingly prolific rose producing clusters of rosette-shaped blooms with masses of petals foiled by dark glossy foliage.

Crimson 'Dortmund' – Shiny foliage graces the abundant single blooms and great autumn hip production.

Dark mauve 'Rhapsody-in-Blue' – Stunning fragrance, exceedingly healthy, free-flowering and well-branched to cover a smaller archway.

Dark pink 'Laguna' – Fragrant, highly recommended rose, which is almost totally resistant to blackspot

Dark red 'Guinea' – Darkest red, fragrant and totally free-flowering rose which is suitable to climb over a huge archway.

Gold 'Golden Celebration' – Luscious large blooms with high fragrance; blooms freely throughout the season.

Gold-red 'Joseph's Coat' – Masses of blooms continually and seriously eye-catching magnificence!

Lemon-white 'Lamarque' – Lemon-centred pure white blooms. Blooms continually; fragrant; glorious, very healthy, mid-green foliage.

Top left: Golden Celebration

Top right: Westerland

Bottom left: Joseph's Coat

Bottom right: Nahema

Mauve 'Jasmina' – Free-flowering, fragrant, nostalgic old-world-shaped blooms. Blooms continually with stunningly healthy foliage.

Mid-pink 'Pinkie' – One of the most floriferous climbing roses, thornless canes with dense and lush mid-green, very healthy foliage.

Orange 'Westerland' – Fragrant blooms which open to display the stamens and shiny, dark green, very healthy foliage.

Pale pink 'Nahema' – Highly fragrant large, deeply cupped flowers. Blooms continually with lots of canes and mid-green healthy foliage.

Pure white 'Iceberg' – Very prolific blooming throughout the season with mid-green, healthy foliage and very few thorns.

Red 'Sympathie' – Very free flowering and very healthy with medium-sized blooms in clusters.

Red-and-white striped 'Fourth Of July' – Single blooms in free-flowering clusters with thorny stems and lush, healthy foliage.

Pink-and-white striped 'Guy Savoy' – The most robust, healthy, happy-smiling rose, which flowers profusely from the ground upwards.

Yellow 'Gold Bunny' – The first and last to flower with huge clusters of medium-sized flowers continually throughout the season.

All of these highly recommended climbers will grow to no less than 3x3m (10x10ft) and can be used on arches or pergolas or espaliered on walls and fences.

Top: Gold Bunny climber
Bottom: Fourth of July

Rambling Roses

Most rambling roses only flower in spring, with some repeat flowering in the autumn. The ramblers deserve a place in the garden where space permits them to show off all their glory because they will cover no less than 10m (33ft) of area and for six weeks in the spring and early summer you will experience the pure bliss, romance and magnificence which rambling roses deliver. Clusters of hips will follow the flowering in autumn on some ramblers if they are left unpruned. The following ramblers are worth consideration:

Albertine – Swirled mass of large pink-apricot blooms in proliferation on a thorny, healthy and rampant rose.

Alberic Barbier – Fragrant clusters of lemon-centred white blooms foiled by dark green, very glossy foliage with good repeat flowering throughout the season.

Mme. Gregoire Staechlin – Highly fragrant, mid-pink waved petal blooms of extraordinary beauty and large bulbous hips in autumn.

Veilchenblau – Dark mauve clusters with yellow stamens adorn the rambler so that you can barely see the foliage when in full flower. Produces glorious hips in autumn.

Wedding Day – Masses of pure white single blooms in clusters; lush, glossy, healthy foliage on very thorny canes; and lovely hips in autumn.

Above: Mme. Gregoire Staechlin

Mermaid – Large, single cream blooms adorn this massive rambling rose spasmodically throughout the season on dark wood with lethal reverse-hooked thorns.

Pillar Roses

The following varieties of pillar rose are suitable for adorning fences or walls, they can be tied to a single pole to add height in the rose garden or they can be free-standing large shrubs in a corner as they reach to around 2½m (8ft) in height and produce canes which have a fan-like growth habit:

Dublin Bay – The most free-flowering pillar rose with continual, glowing red, lightly fragrant blooms; extremely healthy!

Left: Dublin Bay   *Right: Mermaid*

High Hopes – Mid-pink perfectly shaped blooms which appear continually throughout the season; light fragrance; suitable for the vase.

Pierre de Ronsard – Heavy cream petals with pink edges; blooms throughout the season; almost no fragrance unfortunately.

Teasing Georgia – Clotted-creamy yellow/apricot blooms in flushes of magnificence when splayed on a wall.

Altissimo – Bright red, single blooms with yellow stamens; a real 'in-your-face' spectacle in the rose garden.

Top left: High Hopes

Top right: Altissimo
Bottom right: Twilight Glow

Twilight Glow – Huge pale apricot blooms; blooms continually; luscious mid-green very healthy foliage.

Cymbeline – A swirling mass of grey-pink blooms throughout the season; very highly fragrant blooms.

Thornless or near-thornless climbing rose varieties

Crepuscule – Apricot
Renae – Pale pink
Pinkie – Mid-pink
Iceberg – Pure white
Mme. Alfred Carriere – Blush white
Veilchenblau – Dark purple

Selecting the right climbing rose for the
purpose which you intended may require consultation with a rosarian. It is one area of rose selection where choosing the right variety is essential in order to perfectly match it to the specification you require, which might be:

- To protect your yard from intruders – use really thorny varieties.
- To screen your garden from neighbours – use a climbing/rambling rose which produces the most lush, healthy foliage and masses of flowers where possible.
- To create a shade screen for the dog-run or aviary requires a climber which has dense, healthy foliage and preferably fragrant flowers all season. As you will be frequently visiting the pets it's a good idea to plant a most stunning climber in this zone.
- A rambling rose can be perfect for rapidly covering an unsightly structure. It may be that the rose will only flower for a short time in late spring and early summer but the rampant growth will cover the structure very quickly.
- To enjoy the romantic vision of an arch spilling with fragrant roses.
- To shade and cool a seating area under a pergola.

Managing climbing roses is ultimately about you 'being the boss' and remembering that you do have a pair of secateurs and probably sharp loppers too. Use them. Bend, tie and cut the climbers to suit the shape and size you want the plant to be or to cover, whatever structure or form it is you have in your garden. The rewards are immense.

Tips
- *Select the right climbing rose for your specific situation.*
- *'Be the boss' in managing climbing roses.*
- *Well-positioned climbing roses can create the backbone of the garden.*
- *There are a few prolifically flowering thornless roses.*

2.11 Archway for Climbing Roses

If you would love to create a beautiful archway covered in climbing roses, the archway should have a span (width) of no less than 2m (6.5ft) and wider if space permits. Unless it is at least that wide, it would hardly be considered an archway because ideally people should be able to walk two abreast when passing through it.

The arch should be constructed for permanence. Flimsy light-metal objects which come in a flat pack and need to be pushed or screwed together are not ideal for most climbing roses and will probably only last for a few years at best. Climbing roses are really large plants which produce thick canes from the crown (the base of the rose) and the more you tie down and bend those canes, the more profusely the climbing rose will flower.

Steel is a very permanent, durable material and highly recommended for the construction of your archway. Yes, it will definitely be the most expensive option, but hopefully it will still be standing and flowering when you are long gone.

Thick rose canes can be tied to a steel structure using double-sided Velcro or other suitable plant-tie material. Never tie directly around the rose cane or you will cause ring-barking and the branch will die.

Thick chunks of treated pine timber with steel mesh securely screwed in position between the poles may also create a beautiful structure if professionally built and installed. Timber lattice is not suitable, as the staples holding the lattice in place will be pushed out by thick canes that are produced naturally and very early in the development of a climbing rose.

2.12 *The Art of Growing Standard Roses*

Standard roses are such a sight to behold, so stately and grand. A row of the same variety or a row of mixed colours of standard roses creates a very majestic sight in a garden when they are beautifully grown and well staked, as they deserve to be.

Unfortunately, we frequently see standard roses all crooked and bent or planted in the wrong location. Poor sites include up against the eaves of the house or too close to the boundary fence where they will end up tall rather than beautifully rounded as they were created to grow.

Standard roses are an investment in the rose garden landscape – they are more expensive than bush roses because the rose grower endures quite a tedious and lengthy process in order to create them. This is how a standard rose is produced…

A regular standard rose is around 90cm (33in) tall, so thick, straight stems of 1.2m (4ft) of rootstock are harvested and all the eyes (growth points) removed, leaving just three eyes at the top of the cane. The canes are bundled and heeled in aged sawdust so that callousing occurs at the base of the

Above: Sturdy arch for roses

rootstock while the three eyes at the top start to grow. Once the base is calloused, the canes are planted out in the field where they are individually staked and left to grow for nearly six months prior to budding season in early summer.

There are usually two identical varieties of buds implanted on the standard rose rootstock stem – one on either side to create a lovely rounded shape when the rose is mature. Some growers insure the budding success by implanting three buds evenly spaced around the stem because the newly growing buds are very susceptible in high wind and if only one bud remains to mature after a severe weather event, the standard rose may take a few years to create a lovely rounded head.

When the newly inserted buds are growing well, the grower removes the piece of rootstock above them. All the sap and energy flowing along the stem now goes directly to the two or three buds and they start to grow rapidly.

The standard rose is maintained in the field for another 18 months after which time it will be dug up and sold as a two-year-old bare-rooted winter standard rose.

Not every rose variety is suitable for budding onto a standard rose cane because the desired effect is a round-shaped ball of roses. Floribundas, modern shrubs, a few of the David Austin English roses, some old-fashioned roses and Hybrid Teas which have good branching habit make lovely standard rose specimens. Most miniature roses look lovely when budded as standards.

Tall, upright growing varieties of roses are not suitable as standard roses because they are very susceptible to wind damage no matter how well they are staked.

Above: Busy Bee standard

How to Stake a Standard Rose

After such a lengthy growing process, standard roses deserve to be very well staked and grown so that you can revel in their stately beauty for many years in your garden. Since the stake will be positioned to support the standard rose for the life of the rose, we use and recommend steel square tube or round galvanised pipe because wooden tomato stakes will rot within two years leaving the standard rose very vulnerable to bending in the wind and possibly snapping.

Importantly, the stake should extend between 20–30cm (9–12in) above the crown or bud union (point where the branches start to come away from the main stem). This extended piece of stake lends support to the new thick water shoots that are produced from the bud union and are quite vulnerable until they have hardened up. These soft new branches can be loosely tied to the stake, lending them extra support until they harden, most especially if you live in a high-wind zone.

The standard rose should be firmly tied right next to the single steel stake with the top tie being most important. Two or three ties along the stem in the early life of the standard rose will ensure that the stem grows beautifully straight.

The ties should be firm and NEVER be tied around the actual standard rose cane, but rather tied around the stake very firmly then the stem incorporated.

There are many different types of materials used for tying standard roses to their support stake but we use and highly recommend double-sided Velcro tape which will withstand extreme heat and cold, will not perish for many years and offers

Above: Staking a standard rose

absolute security that the standard rose stem will not be compromised but remain firmly attached to the stake for many years.

NEVER TIE A STANDARD OR WEEPING ROSE TO THE STAKE WITH WIRE OR ELECTRIC CABLE TIE AS IT WILL RING-BARK THE ROSE WITHIN A SEASON

Regular maintenance of the ties is imperative because the standard rose stem thickens with age when planted in the open ground. Every three months or so, make it part of your rose garden maintenance agenda to check the ties on the standard roses. Release the tie, move it slightly up or down the stem so that moisture or small bugs are removed and securely re-tie.

Too frequently we are asked to supply a replacement, well-established standard rose because one in a row was blown over in the wind. Adequately staking and tying standard roses is imperative and must be constantly maintained.

Left: Old bark   *Right: City of Newcastle standard*

Weeping roses

All of the above staking and tying criteria applies to supporting a weeping rose. However, a weeping rose must have a metal ring bolted to the top of a galvanised steel pole to encourage the rose canes to weep outwards and then fall downwards.

The ring and pole kit must be constructed of high-grade steel because a beautiful quality weeping rose will produce lots of thick branches and water shoots, which carry heavy clusters of flowers. Some varieties of weeping roses will easily cover a steel Australian designed washing line.

As standard and weeping roses age, their stem thickens, the bark on the stems may crack and fall just like on old tree trunks. Just as humans get shorter and frequently a bit wider in the girth as they get older, the roses shrink in the length of their stem and these

Left: A 30-year-old standard rose

Right: Standard roses grown too close to a window

30-year-old standard roses would originally have had 90cm (35in) stems about 2cm (¾in) thick. The stems are now less than 60cm (24in) tall but they are 12–15cm (5–6in) thick.

Most varieties of standard and weeping roses flower for more than eight months each season and will give you immense pleasure for many, many years. Providing adequate support for them is absolutely crucial to the success and longevity of the planting.

Tips
- *Never use wire or electric cable tie on any roses.*
- *Standard rose stems thicken and get shorter with age.*
- *Adequate support for the life of the standard is imperative.*
- *Not all roses are suitable for budding as standards.*

2.13 Growing Roses in Containers

With smaller gardens and more people wanting to create gardens in courtyards and on balconies, it is increasingly popular to grow roses in containers. This can be very rewarding and successful if you follow these simple instructions:
- Use only high-quality potting mix which is guaranteed to have added nutrients and water-saving properties;
- Buy large pots or containers rather than lots of small pots as this ensures greater longevity in moisture retention;
- Re-pot roses at least every two years, ideally during winter when you should also prune the roots;
- Place containers planted with roses in an open, sunny location;
- Water daily – in extremely hot weather, place a saucer under the pot to ensure the potting mix isn't completely dry all the time;
- Water over the entire rose plant at least fortnightly with a liquid seaweed solution;
- Apply monthly applications of the organic rose spray maintenance program to keep pests and disease at bay;

- Once a month feed the roses with complete organic fertilizer granules because the fertilizer drains more quickly due to regular watering;
- Plant herbs, vegetables and annual flowers around the base of roses in tubs to shade the potting mix from drying out too quickly;
- Self-watering containers are ideal for growing roses because the roots have a constant supply of moisture and nutrients available.

Decorator pots look stunning with healthy flowering roses in them. However, many of these pots are very porous. Terracotta is more porous than concrete. To overcome this, you might consider planting the rose into a plastic pot before placing into the decorator pot. Fill around the base, sides and top of the pot with potting mix or fine-grade mulch that will act as an insulator, keeping the roots moist and cool to reduce the need for constant watering.

Climbing Roses in Containers. Every rose is quite suited to being grown in a container. Just don't try and grow a 2m (6.5ft) high climbing rose in a 30cm (12in) pot because the pot size will restrict root growth, which will in turn limit the size of the climbing rose.

For a climbing rose to reach its maximum height and width potential in a container, use a very large tub like a half wine barrel with drain holes drilled in the base. Climbing roses can most definitely grow huge and cover large areas, even when they are grown in pots in a paved courtyard.

Consider drilling large holes in the base

Above: Self watering container

of the pot or even completely remove the base of the container to allow the rose roots to penetrate the surrounding soil zone. To achieve growth over a large pergola or similar, remove a few pavers so that the pot rests directly on the soil which subsequently reduces the high maintenance factor of daily watering. The rose roots will go down into the soil under the pavers and grow into a really fine specimen and it will definitely not lift pavers.

This technique works particularly well where you want the thorny canes up off ground level in a courtyard that is used as a family play area or where your pets need to exercise without restriction.

If it is not possible for the climbing rose to send roots down into the soil, the size of the climber will be severely restricted by the size of the container. A medium-sized climbing rose when planted into open ground will achieve a height of more than 3m (10ft) but will grow less than 2m (6.5ft) tall and wide with its roots restricted to the size of a half wine barrel which is sitting on concrete or pavers.

Standard Roses in Containers still need to be staked when they are in a pot. The container should be a heavy one so that it doesn't blow over in the wind. Maximum height for a standard or maybe even a short weeping rose in a container is around 1.2m (4ft) because the risk of breaking in the wind, growing too top heavy and canes snapping jeopardises the success of such planting.

Keeping a standard rose in a pot for a number of years will naturally reduce the ability of the stem thickening to the extent that it otherwise would do if planted into the open garden so it is prudent to repot the standard rose at least every two years, each time increasing the size of the container or ultimately plant the standard rose into the open garden soil.

Above: Climber in tub nursery

Standard Roses in Containers. Standard Roses still need to be staked when they are in a pot. The container should be a heavy one so that it doesn't blow over in the wind. Maximum height for a standard or maybe even a short weeping rose in a container is around 1.2m (4ft) because the risk of breaking in the wind, growing too top heavy and canes snapping jeopardises the success of such planting.

Keeping a standard rose in a pot for a number of years will naturally reduce the ability of the stem thickening to the extent that it otherwise would do if planted into the open garden so it is prudent to repot the standard rose at least every two years, each time increasing the size of the container or ultimately plant the standard rose into the open garden soil.

Other Roses in Containers. Because some varieties of roses will be impossible to repot every couple of years, since their roots are imbedded into the surrounding soil, it will be essential to regenerate the potting medium by carefully removing some soil from all around the roots in the top of the pot to replace it with high quality compost and potting medium.

Alternatively, core holes into the root zone and fill those with high quality compost, fertilizer pellets and water in with liquid seaweed. This task should be carried out in winter when the rose is dormant. Cutting some of the roots away as well as pruning the growth can be very invigorating to the potted rose and it will continue to flourish for many years.

Patio and Miniature Roses in Containers. Patio and miniature roses make a fantastic display, they are fun and really easy to grow in smaller sized containers as they are generally grown on their own roots, not grafted. These roses are a wonderful way of enticing children to become interested in growing roses. They learn to respect the prickles on roses and because patio and miniature roses repeat flower so frequently, the kids are rewarded for their efforts and stay interested.

Potted patio and miniature roses can be used as table-centre decorations for a few days at a time in a light, sunny room. Pop them in the house when you have guests or a special occasion then put them back outdoors where they will be far less susceptible to pests and disease due to lack of sunlight and good air-flow while the rose is inside the house.

Tips
- *After years in a container, consider planting your rose in the ground.*
- *Use self-watering pots if you go away regularly.*
- *Growth habit of every rose will be restricted according to pot size.*
- *Feed more regularly as fertilizer is leached through potting mix.*

2.14 *What to Plant Around Roses*

The appearance of your rose garden will be enhanced by planting lots of other plants amongst the roses, they will also be beneficial by attracting a host of predator insects. Herbs like garlic and parsley will deter aphids while spring-flowering daffodils and other flowers will encourage early breeding of ladybirds by providing necessary food for them. Plant lots of annuals around the border of the rose garden using a different colour theme each season to create excitement and to deter the lawn from invading the rose garden.

All sorts of perennials with spires of striking colours look sensational around roses; they also cover and shade the soil, keeping it cool and moist just as mulch would. Because roses require adequate ventilation to prevent fungal disease, regularly pruning perennials when they've finished flowering and generally keeping them in check by pulling them out from around the base of roses is imperative in order to maintain healthy rose foliage. Lots of seasonal vegetables like silver beet, tomatoes, corn and even potatoes can be grown in the rose garden to make very productive use of the space underneath and between rose bushes. Vegetables will also benefit from the organic rose maintenance spray to keep them pest and disease free whilst enhancing crop yields.

Standard roses allow a lot of area underneath to plant low-growing herbs, vegetables, bulbs, annuals and perennials.

In one of my own garden beds, which is 12m (40ft) long and 3m (10ft) deep, there are 25 bush roses, two short weeping roses and six standard roses planted with clumps of silver beet, calendula, aquilegia, hellebores, anemones, peonies, geraniums, poppies, lilies and daffodils. For seasonal variety I threw in seeds of nasturtium, which was ultimately a big mistake as they grew too wildly and, because of their brightness, dominated all the other beautiful colours in the garden.

Some perennials should be removed before they seed because they grow too densely around the lower bush roses and if there is evidence of mildew on the rose foliage, it's an indication that the airflow around the roses is inadequate and the perennials should be trimmed.

Because of the variety of plants used in this particular garden bed, it always looks interesting, there is always something flowering and I can make a vase arrangement of flowers for inside at a minute's notice.

Left: Veg/Rose Garden   *Right: Duet and Anemone*

As the garden is very close to the house, I use it as a place where a 'rescued' or 'gifted' plant can be popped in without thought or concern for colour compatibility; it can always be shifted to another part of the garden. There is no planning or design for such a garden – it evolves and is constantly changing, which also makes it very functional.

A climbing rose is almost incomplete without its most glorious companion, hybrid clematis. On their own, hybrid clematis seem to flounder and look rather 'daggy' but plant one right next to a climbing rose and it scrambles through the rose, clinging to the branches whilst enhancing the magnificence of the rose.

They enjoy the same conditions and revel in each other's company because the climbing rose provides shade and a cool, moist root-zone, which is imperative to ensure healthy vigour of hybrid clematis. Together, they are breathtakingly sensational.

Be adventurous and enjoy lots of different plants around your roses. A purist might gasp at your colour combinations but you can be sure that God is smiling.

Tips
- *Roses are great companions to nearly every other plant except large trees.*
- *Standard roses afford great space underneath for season colour variation.*
- *Grow seasonal vegetables amongst the roses.*
- *Be adventurous and plant lots of colour around the rose garden.*

2.15 Cutting Roses for the Vase

For around eight months each year you can produce a steady supply of rose flowers for use as cut flowers to decorate your home. This is a great incentive to grow roses in the home garden and the most suitable rose type to use is the classic Hybrid Tea, which produces long-stemmed roses that are, with careful selection, very often highly fragrant.

Rose blooms picked from healthy, well-watered plants should remain fresh in the vase for many days providing you take a bucket of water out to the garden with you so that the blooms are dunked within moments of being picked.

The stage at which the bloom is picked for presentation in the vase depends on the variety. Big blowsy Hybrid Teas like 'Just Joey' should be harvested when they are well on the way to fully opening as the buds will not open otherwise. Bracts of the five-petal blooms of 'Sally Holmes' or 'Rosendorf Sparrieshoop' should be cut when the first flowers on the stem are fully opened and the whole bract will continue to open during the next week or more.

Floribundas and modern shrubs are best picked when three or more flowers are fully opened on the stem so the side buds will slowly open thereafter. This showy home decoration is enhanced when the petals start to fall around the base of the vase.

When you cut a rose stem from the bush, air is immediately sucked into the stem and it's this trapped air in the leaves and stems of the flowers that causes them to wilt, even after they are placed in water. Conditioning the flowers to enjoy their lasting qualities in a vase can rectify this.

Left: Fresh and old blooms of Sally Holmes *Right: Sally Holmes cluster*

Once you've picked the flowers, fill the bucket to the brim and place it in a cool dark place for a few hours to stop evaporation. A household refrigerator temperature is too cold to store a bucket of cut rose blooms so the coolest place in the house is usually the bathroom or laundry.

When you are ready to start arranging the flowers, add a sachet of Chrysal (flower preservative) to each 2 litres (4 pints) of water in the vase. At this point, the leaves should feel firm when you remove the lowest ones from the stems before placing them in the vase. There is no need to rush with arranging because you have conditioned the flowers and their stems will be filled with water rather than air.

If the roses are wilted, as may happen despite immediate dunking in water, you can restore them by using three tablespoons of sugar dissolved in hot water. Hot water contains less air than cold water. When you submerge the rose stem into hot water, it is absorbed all the way up the stem, driving out the air bubbles that caused it to wilt. Sugar also acts as food for the cut flowers.

To avoid needing to change the water every day, I always add 5ml of Sanitiser (Hydrogen Peroxide 6 per cent) to every litre (2 pints) of water in the vase and provided there are no leaves in the water, many of the long-stemmed Hybrid Tea roses will last at least 10 days by changing the water every three or four days.

Floribundas or cluster-flowered roses, modern shrub roses, even climbing roses which may only have five petals can all be used as cut flowers and providing you treat them as recommended, they will decorate your home in vases for many days.

Some varieties of roses, especially the David Austin and old-fashioned roses

Above: Frog and fallen rose petals

which can have more than 70 petals in each flower, fail to last as a cut flower despite all the conditioning you offer. Float them in an open pasta bowl or small fishbowl to use as a table centrepiece. Adding a floating candle adds special romance to the bowl.

A smart man brought home a gift of five magnificent rose bushes for his wife, which she planted and carefully tended in their garden. She loved to pick the blooms and always had vases of beautiful, fragrant roses in their home. One day she complained that he never brought her flowers and he responded "But honey, I bought you a rose garden." This very smart man would be even smarter if he came home with a lovely bunch of florist roses during winter.

Enjoy vases of roses in your home throughout the flowering season and you will be doing your roses a huge favour by constantly cutting long stems so that the rose will be kept neat and tidy while continually producing an abundance of strong, healthy stems to enable you to do it all over again, and again and again.

Above (both images): Cutting blooms to display in vases enhances the home and is good for the plants

2.16 Rose Propagation in the Home Garden

Of course you can take cuttings from your roses and create new bushes to either plant in your own garden or take down to the local school fete, street stall or garden club meeting to share with friends. Taking cuttings is rewarding and fun for rose enthusiasts and your children will love to do it too.

Just remember that some varieties of roses are easier to propagate than others and this is the main reason why nearly all roses in commercial production are budded onto rose understock to ensure their longevity and hardiness.

Many varieties of new release roses are protected by PBR (Plant Breeders Rights) so that the rose breeder is financially rewarded for creating the new rose and such protected roses should never be sold without a plant label.

Take cuttings from all different types and colours of roses. Be sure not to fill your rose garden with the same particular variety of rose just because you are successful at taking cuttings of that rose. Your rose garden will soon become very uninteresting!

If you have a rose that has extreme significance and you've tried to take cuttings but haven't been successful, contact your local Rose Society or a specialist rose nursery for advice. The rose may well be in commercial production and very easy to buy.

However, if the rose is unable to be positively identified as being in commercial production, sending bud wood to a rose grower to have it 'contract budded' during spring/summer can be a good way to propagate it.

There are many various methods used to propagate roses and I recommend that you take cuttings and try all the methods at different times of the season, but most definitely during autumn because the days are cooler with plenty of sunshine and roses grow particularly well in autumn. At least one of these methods should result in a successful 'take'.

The most common method is to take a piece of stem from where the rose has flowered and, before it starts sending out new shoots, cut stems about pencil thick, 20cm (8in) long, leaving a few leaves at the top and poke them into the ground at the base of the existing rose. If the soil is moist and conditions are in your favour, the cutting should strike. Leave it there for a couple of months until you are sure it has good root development then lift it, plant it into quality potting mix and leave it in a sheltered but sunny location for several weeks. Keep it moist but not sopping wet.

Layering is also possible. Bend a branch over, press it down with a wire hook or put a stone on it and cover it with soil. When the cutting has taken, chop the branch that is attached to the original plant. Lift the cutting or if using this method to cover a fence-line or to create a hedge, leave the cutting to grow and take a layer from it to create another plant. It would take quite a number of years to achieve a dense hedgerow of roses by this method of propagation but it would eventually be magnificent and very rewarding.

A more certain method of striking cuttings is to set up a polystyrene box with drainage

Left: Cutting with lowest leaves removed   *Right: Rose cutting*

holes in the base, add high quality seed-raising mix to about half-way and find or make a cover of clear glass or plastic. Pop name labels at the end of each row of cuttings. Moisten the soil with liquid seaweed and insert cuttings of different lengths and thickness. Place the cover on and put the box in a warm, sheltered position in the garden.

Check the box every couple of days without lifting the lid, in order to retain warmth and moisture. Only add water if absolutely necessary because most cuttings fail because they are over-watered. Add liquid seaweed to the water to stimulate root development if the potting medium feels extremely dry – probably do this only once every couple of weeks under normal conditions.

This method of rose propagation can be used when you may need to take cuttings during spring or summer, when the rose material is 'soft-wood'. Cut the bottom corners off a zip-lock food storage bag which has seedling mix or potting mix with added Vermiculite or Perlite and thoroughly wet the medium with liquid seaweed solution.

Close the zip-lock bag and hang it to drain for a couple of hours. In the meantime, take cuttings from a rose stem that has flowered. Remove the base two or three leaf nodes. It is vitally important to retain leaves on the uppermost two leaf nodes, as leafless pieces are less likely to succeed.

Re-cut the stem of the cutting and dip immediately into rooting hormone powder (or honey) before placing three or four cuttings almost to the bottom of the zip-lock bag. Seal the bag and write the name of the rose on the front of the bag with a permanent marker.

When taking lots of cuttings, place the bags upright in a moderately warm, sunny location where there is no direct sunlight and where they will not be disturbed while they are developing roots. Open the bags occasionally to remove mouldy leaves or dead cuttings and re-seal immediately. Moisture droplets should be evident on the inside of the bags and only ever add a teaspoon of water if you consider it absolutely necessary.

Soon enough you will see root development at the base of the bag. Let the roots develop until they are very clearly visible then leave the bag open for a couple of days to allow the cuttings to harden off – they may need a little liquid seaweed solution because the mix must not dry out at this vital stage in the creation of a new rose.

Gently remove the cuttings from the bag by scooping out a handful of soil around the roots and place them into 10–15cm (4–6in) pots. Water in with weak liquid seaweed solution and place in a sheltered, filtered-light location. Check the soil before watering again because the new roots need a balance of air and moisture and the baby plants will die if overwatered at this stage. As the plants gain substance and start to grow leaves, move them into full sunlight and apply weak liquid seaweed solution weekly.

The organic rose management spray program should be introduced as soon as leaves appear and then applied fortnightly to ensure no fungal disease invades the cuttings. Remove all dropped foliage and keep the area around the pots well aerated. Plant the cuttings into the ground when well established.

Another way of propagating roses is to harvest the hips (seed pods) in autumn, wait for them to mature or immediately open the hips, remove the seeds and plant them into seed-raising mixture. Do not overwater and remember to use name labels at the end of each row of seeds so that you have a record of the parent.

Every seedling produced will be a different rose and you just never know, your seedling has the potential to be a great rose which you can name whatever you like and then register your very own rose for commercial production.

Taking cuttings and making new plants is such a creative and rewarding aspect of gardening. Have a go, its great fun!

Above: Cutting in ground
Next spread: Chartreuse de Parme

Part 3: Cultural Notes for Roses

3.17 Position to Plant Roses

Roses need at least five hours of direct sunlight per day during the growing and flowering season. With a good amount of sunlight they will flower profusely while maintaining good health and vigour.

If you're planting a very new garden, be sure to take in the whole environment of the garden before you start planting your roses. Look up and down, then in all directions and think about how this garden will look in a few years' time. Small trees grow into large trees; yes, you can prune the trees to ensure they don't shade your roses but this can become a very expensive exercise if it needs to be professionally managed on an annual basis and this must be taken into consideration at the outset.

Also, be aware that some trees have very invasive root systems which will impose on the performance of your roses – lots of tree species will suck up every bit of nutrient and moisture you apply. I suggest planting roses at least 3m (10ft) away from large trees, or even further away if space permits.

You think the roses are being fed and watered by your diligent applications of fertilizer and water but they are quite likely looking like you don't care about them at all because the trees are taking every bit of your precious caring.

Air circulation around the roses is also very important in order to reduce the potential incidence of disease. The more 'out in the open' the roses are planted, the healthier they will be.

Tips
- *When flowering roses need five hours of direct sunlight daily.*
- *Plant roses away from large trees.*
- *Ensure good air circulation.*

Opposite page: Mass planting Casanova

3.18 Ideal Weather Conditions for Roses

Roses actually **LOVE** hot, dry and sunny weather conditions especially where they have consistently adequate irrigation. Roses flower beautifully throughout spring, summer and autumn. Some varieties will flower during the winter in warm and sunny weather and it is sunshine, direct and available for no less than five hours a day which is a key component to successful rose growing.

Roses are grown and flower well very close to the beach in coastal regions where cold, harsh and salt-laden winds batter them constantly.

Rosa rugosa varieties are the most commonly grown roses in this environment, however many tough-foliaged modern shrubs will also grow and flower continually in such harsh conditions. Coastal gardens will no doubt challenge many rose varieties so careful selection is imperative if you live in such a location.

Left: Iceberg   *Right: Knockout*

Here are just a few modern shrub roses to consider for a coastal garden:

Summer Memories (white)
Knockout series
Bonica (light pink)
Iceberg (and sports)
La Sevillana (bright red)
Topaz Jewel (yellow)
Rosendorf Sparrieshoop (mid-pink)
Flower Carpet series

You can grow roses high up in the mountains where winter snow prevails.

Bottom left: La Sevillana

Top Right: Summer Memories
Bottom Right: Rosendorf Sparrieshoop

The roses will flower later in the spring/early summer, then right through the summer and into autumn. Extreme cold conditions below freezing (5°C or 32°F) to more than -5°C (23°F) for weeks on end may require that the roses be covered with hessian or mulch during winter.

In some very, very cold climates, the roses are actually dug up and buried in big underground pits for the entire winter, or wooden containers are placed over them to protect them until the weather starts to warm.

If you live in a zone with extreme cold and freezing weather conditions, never prune until very late winter or early spring because frost burn can and will kill the roses. In extreme hot weather the flower colour can change. In some of the darker varieties, the colour will intensify.

Pale-coloured rose blooms may actually bleach and some afternoon shade or filtered light from overhead trees would be an advantage to retain colour in those conditions. An example of this is 'Violina' which appears to have creamy/white blooms because it faces the very hot afternoon sun from midday onwards. 'Violina' during the rest of the flowering season is actually deep pink fading to pale pink as it ages.

When doing consultations for the really hot zones, I always highly recommend some bright/strong coloured roses be planted amongst the pastels so that the eye is drawn to take a closer look at a rose garden and it retains interest. This can also be achieved by planting clumps of perennial plants amongst the pastel-coloured roses.

These are just a few varieties that are outstanding performers in very hot weather conditions:

Above: Maurice Utrillo

St. Patrick	Gold Bunny
Double Delight	Lion's Rose
Ebb Tide	Red Intuition

Old-fashioned roses such as Tea Roses perform exceptionally well in a hot climate where they are likely to flower continually throughout the year.

Tropical weather presents the most difficult conditions for rose gardeners because humidity will always encourage fungal problems on rose foliage and the roses will require more frequent applications of the organic rose maintenance spray program in this climate zone. Good ventilation is imperative in a humid environment and will assist in reducing the incidence of fungal disease.

Place a good thick layer of mulch over the garden bed around the roses with a lighter layer around the base of the rose bushes so that when the wind does blow, it blows freely through the lower storey of the plants.

Hygienic garden practice is imperative for gardeners who live in a humid climate. Remove spent blooms constantly as this reduces the amount of petal litter and also ensures that healthy new growth is always happening.

Tips
- *Roses need at least five hours of full sun per day.*
- *Rugosa roses are ideal in seaside locations.*
- *Prune during late winter in very cold zones.*
- *Garden hygiene is imperative in humid conditions.*

Above: Rosette Delizy (tea rose)

3.19 Designing a Rose Garden

You keep looking at a space at the front of your house and dream of a rose garden to fill that area. How do you go about fulfilling that dream? It's not that difficult once you start to put pen to paper and do a sketch of the site, step out the boundary and mark dimensions of the area on the sketch.

On this simple drawing, indicate the aspect of the garden – north, south, east and west. This design indicates north-facing so there will be adequate sunshine with no obstruction of trees or other buildings.

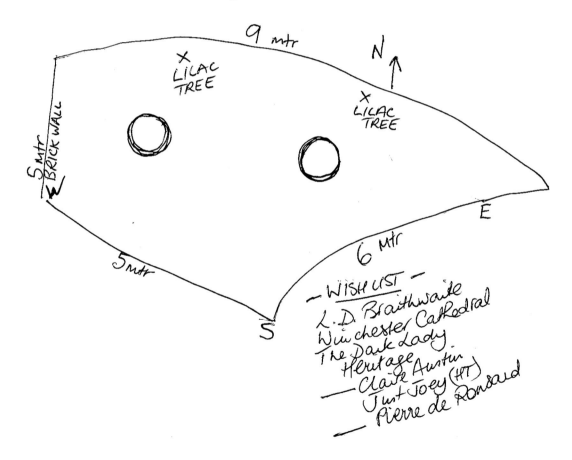

Above: Mud Map

Next, include any existing features like a brick wall on the western boundary, a hedge on a border or there may be trees and other plants which need to be factored into the overall design.

Because roses are generally spaced 1m (3ft) apart, you will now be able to get a rough idea of the number of roses you need. Approximately 30 bush roses will fit this space so you can now start researching the varieties of roses you like and how they might be planted. Should they be in rows, or clumps, should they be taller at the back and shorter towards the front border of the bed? Is fragrance important or are prickles an issue? Do you prefer lots of different colours, or shades of the same colour perhaps?

Write all your priorities on the drawing as you start to refine these specifications including the names of roses that MUST be in the planting.

The original wish list included two climbing roses 'Claire Austin' and 'Pierre de Ronsard' which are both suitable to grow as pillar roses, so they will be positioned in

Left: Gold Bunny   Right: Red Intuition

obelisks centrally located to add a beautiful dimension of height and complement the existing lilac trees which are planted on either side at the back of the garden bed.

Other choices on the wish list are mostly David Austin roses, which lend themselves really well to planting in groups of three roses of the same variety. Such a group of one variety should be planted at 75cm (30in) spacing. The space between each group should be 1.5m (5ft) so that you can easily walk around the garden to pick the blooms and each 'blob' of colour is distinct from the other.

There is adequate space for nine groups with three roses in each group.
Roses selected are all around the same height of 1.2m (4ft) tall:

> L.D. Braithwaite (dr)
> Winchester Cathedral (w)
> The Dark Lady (dp)
> Heritage (lp)
> Just Joey (HT ab)

To complete this garden design, select four more roses of complementary colours and growth habit. My suggestions would be:

> Molineux (ly)
> Peach Profusion (Mod. Shrub ab)
> Pat Austin (ob)
> Munstead Wood (dr)

Place rose variety names on the plan and note down where they will be planted. Before you know it, you have a completed rose garden design.

Tips
- *Keep the design simple.*
- *Check aspect offers no less than five hours direct sun every day.*

Top left: *The Dark Lady*
Bottom left: *Munstead Wood Fully Open*

Top right: *Munstead Wood*
Bottom right: *Molineux*

Top Left: Winchester Cathedral

Bottom Left: Just Joey

Top Right: Heritage

Bottom Right: L.D Braithwaite

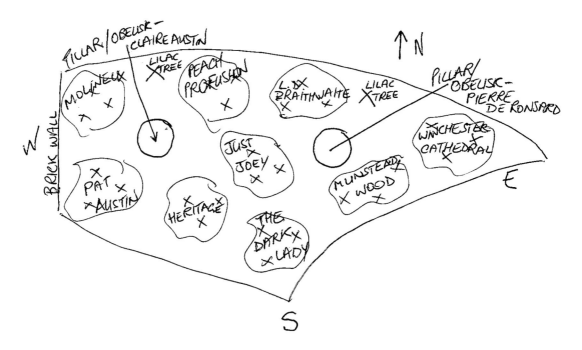

PILLAR/OBELISK—CLAIRE AUSTIN

N ↑

MOLINEUX x

LILAC TREE

PEACH PROFUSION x

L. D. BRAITHWAITE x

LILAC TREE

PILLAR/OBELISK—PIERRE DE RONSARD

W

BRICK WALL

WINCHESTER CATHEDRAL x

JUST JOEY x

PAT AUSTIN x

HERITAGE x

THE DARK LADY x

MUNSTEAD WOOD x

E

S

Top: A completed rose garden design

Bottom left: Pat Austin

Bottom right: Peach Profusion

3.20 Soil for Planting Roses and Fertilizer Explained

Roses flourish in a wide range of soil types. Preparing soil prior to planting by adding well-composted organic materials will guarantee robust, healthy and free-flowering rose bushes for many years.

NEVER remove the existing soil, but rather enhance it by adding loads of composted organic material. This may delay planting by a few months but will be well worth the effort in the overall performance of the roses in the long-term.

Composted organic material is usually a balanced blend of animal manures and food waste, which can be purchased bagged and readily available. You can definitely use your own compost provided it is all well broken down, friable and rather sweet smelling. Never add raw manure into the soil because it will burn plant roots.

The soil must be well drained because roses hate wet feet. To test how well your soil drains, dig a hole and fill it with water. If the water takes many hours to drain away, you probably have a heavy clay soil that can only be improved by adding clay-breaker (gypsum) and lots of organic matter. Planting roses should be delayed until the drainage is improved.

In coastal regions your soil may be very sandy and too well drained. Add lots of organic matter and apply liquid seaweed regularly to improve the water holding capacity of sandy soil. Soil-wetting agents should also be regularly applied, especially if you notice the soil is hydrophobic (water runs over the top rather than down into the soil).

Roses enjoy 6.5 pH (acid/alkaline ratio) and this can be tested using a simple pH test kit. Too much raw animal manure will lower the pH to an acid reading of 5.5 or less, adding dolomite lime will sweeten the soil to increase pH so adding a bit of everything will ensure an average pH of around 6–6.5, which is ideal for growing healthy roses.

Soil is the life force of the rose garden and the more organic materials you add, the greater number of earth worms and soil microbes you will have working to enhance the soil condition and thus provide a dynamic and vibrant source of nutrition for your plants.

Regular applications, no less than once a month, of liquid seaweed will definitely promote soil conditioning and assist in releasing soil nutrients which may be locked-up in the soil however, liquid seaweed is not an adequate fertilizer for the soil so we promote the use of complete organic fertilizer because it contains only natural forms of plant nutrients, which ensure that the plants receive a balanced diet of essential nutrients, as well as delivering high levels of natural humates to improve the structure and performance of the soil. What this means is that you are not really feeding the plants, you are feeding the soil that in turn will provide nutrition for the plants and this is vitally important to a healthy, productive garden.

Complete organic fertilizer is made from a blend of magnesite, reactive phosphate rock, gypsum, humates, lime, bentonite, potassium sulphate, nitrified coal and elemental sulphur. Organic fertilizer does not have to stink for days after it has been applied – in fact, it should not smell at all if it is high quality, very well composted and contain humus.

Humus is derived from the breakdown, under the right bacterial conditions, of organic matter whose origins have come from decomposed green vegetation. It is a valuable source of humic acid, the salts of which are known as humates.

Humates, as the active ingredients in the soil's organic matter, play a critical role in soil fertility as they hold nutrients and release them over time as plants require them. Humates will improve the soil structure, helping it to breathe and hold moisture, which allows rose roots to penetrate the soil deeply.

Roses will readily take up the nutrients in humate-rich fertilizer so that less fertilizer is required to maintain healthy, vibrant bushes with a higher resistance to insects, disease and extremely cold or hot weather conditions. The plants will respond by producing a greater number of strong-stemmed, long-lasting flowers over a longer period.

Chemical or synthetic fertilizer is water-

Above: Worms are essential for healthy soil

soluble and is therefore taken up by plants whether they need the nutrition or not, and this can overload the plant. In the case of roses, this will create lots of very sappy, lush foliage that is very appealing to insects like aphids and it will also reduce the number of large, quality blooms because the plant is busy creating and supporting all the lush foliage.

Organic fertilizer should contain a balance of major (NPK) nutrients with trace elements and have an approximate analysis which reads something like:

(N) Nitrogen	3.2%
(P) Phosphorous	3.2%
(K) Potassium	3.3%
Sulphur	10.0%
Calcium	13.0%
Magnesium	2.6%

With so many fertilizer products available, take your time, read the packaging and source a quality organic blend to sprinkle over the entire soil area of the rose garden. Roses spread feeder roots around the entire growth canopy so a large old-fashioned shrub or climber will require more fertilizer than a small Floribunda or Miniature rose on the border of the garden.

Light applications frequently is the key to successful soil nurturing and an average application of one-handful per bush every eight weeks throughout the year will adequately support and maintain healthy, free-flowering rose bushes.

If you produce your own compost, place this around the base of the roses and cover with mulch to preserve the microbes. Your compost will be a welcome compliment to an organic fertilizer program so your soil will be teeming with earthworms and soil microbes.

Tips
- *Roses grow well when soil pH is 6–6.5.*
- *Prepare the soil prior to planting roses.*
- *Use lots of composted organic material around roses.*
- *You are feeding the soil not the plants.*

3.21 Preparing a New Rose Bed

The most successful and rewarding rose gardens are those where the soil was well prepared prior to planting and autumn is the ideal season to prepare your new garden beds for winter planting of bare-rooted roses.

Remove the grass/weeds to a depth of about 5–10cm (2–4in). This 'turf' can be laid in another area to create a lawn or place it on the compost heap upside down where it will break down and provide compost for another garden bed once the weeds are 'cooked'.

Do not dig the cleared area because it is backbreaking work and there is no need for you to do it. There is an army of workers waiting underground for you to proceed to the next step of creating this new rose bed and they will happily do all the necessary digging and aerating which is essential to create a well-drained site suitable for bare-rooted roses.

Apply gypsum and liquid seaweed over the area then pile on any combination of animal manures or whatever composted material is available. Take some litter from under a range of shrubs and trees in other areas of your garden and spread them over the compost. This will supply mycorrhiza (fungi) from your own garden environment and is an integral component in the soil life when preparing a new garden bed. Lightly mulch with lucerne or pea straw and water weekly if there is no rain.

Sprinkle rock dust and liquid sea minerals to ensure a balanced range of earth and sea minerals are incorporated into the soil.

Liquid seaweed applied weekly will act as a soil conditioner as well as feed the worms, your army of workers without whom your garden will not flourish at all. They will rapidly come to the surface and begin aerating the soil for you. As they chew their way through all the manure, straw, leaf litter and goodness you've been adding to the site, they will generously add their castings to the soil. If the pile of manure you have applied rots down to become humus and the bed needs to be raised, keep adding more manure and straw layers up to four weeks prior to planting.

When you are ready to plant the roses, the only area to dig will be at the planting hole. By doing this, you reduce weed activation because you are not disturbing the soil structure of the entire garden bed.

Tips
- *Prepare new rose beds six weeks prior to planting.*
- *Reduce weeds – only dig at the planting holes.*
- *Liquid seaweed is a great soil conditioner.*
- *Worms are your army of workers.*

3.22 Seasonal Rose Planting and Transplanting

Planting Bare-rooted Roses in Winter. You've pored over rose catalogues and changed your mind a million times, but finally selected the varieties to be planted in the new garden. The rose bed has looked empty for weeks while waiting for this grand moment.

The new roses should still be packaged, or they might already have been soaking in a weak liquid seaweed solution for a few hours. The roots should NEVER dry out during this critical time – leave the roses soaking in buckets or troughs throughout the planting process.

Using a garden fork (so you don't slice though all the worms who've been aerating and casting into the soil), dig a rough-walled hole at least 50x50cm (20x20in) to adequately accommodate and spread out the rose roots. Remove soil from the planting hole and poke holes in the base and walls to enable roots to immediately start penetrating deeply into the soil.

DO NOT ADD FERTILIZER OR ANIMAL MANURE.

Remove the rose from the packaging and dip in seaweed solution. Prune off any broken roots and give the rose stems a trim to outward facing buds.

Create a mound of soil in the hole and spread the rose roots down over the mound and start backfilling the soil, making sure you keep the crown above the soil. With your foot, firmly press the soil around the neck of the rose to create a well, water thoroughly to create a slurry of mud to expel any air around the roots. Add light soil or bagged compost to fill the well so the crown is just above the existing soil level, which allows space for a light application of milled lucerne mulch or pea straw.

Soak the entire area thoroughly with no less than 10 litres (21 pints) of water to which liquid seaweed has been added. Unless it rains, the new rose will require at least 10 litres (21 pints) of water weekly.

If there is heavy rain and you notice the rose is sitting in a puddle of water constantly, lift it out of the ground and place it in a pot until the drainage problem is rectified before replanting. Roses hate wet feet and bare-rooted roses will perish very quickly if left in soggy ground.

Planting a Potted Flowering Rose. If you, like me, prefer to plant new roses in the garden after they have established in a pot, you can do this at any time of the year, even in extremely hot weather provided you offer adequate irrigation to the newly planted rose which has been pampered with daily watering while potted.

Using a garden fork, dig a rough-walled hole at least 50x50cm (20x20in) for a 30cm (12in) pot. The size of the planting hole must be at least 10cm (4in) wider than the pot so that friable soil can be placed around the wall of the root-ball to allow new roots immediate access to soil moisture and nutrients.

Remove soil from the planting hole and poke holes in the base and walls. Fill the hole with water to which liquid seaweed has been added. Allow to drain.

DO NOT ADD FERTILIZER OR ANIMAL MANURE.

To remove the rose from the pot, lie it sideways on the ground and gently squeeze on the pot. When you turn it back up, the rose should easily lift out of the container.

Immediately set the rose in the hole without unnecessarily disturbing the roots. The potting mix level should sit just below the existing soil level so there is space to push friable soil and mulch over the potting mix. It is very important that the potting mix is not exposed or the rose will dry out and perish.

Tamp the soil down with your foot to create a shallow well. Completely drench the soil to remove any pockets of air around the root-ball. Pour 10 litres (21 pints) of liquid seaweed solution over the entire plant to reduce transplanting shock and don't water again for a couple of days.

In extremely hot weather, any flowers on the bush may wilt so trim the flowers and put them in a vase. Be sure to leave lots of foliage on the newly planted rose to provide the stems with adequate protection from sunburn.

Apply liquid seaweed fortnightly and fertilize after 6–8 weeks with complete organic fertilizer.

Transplanting an Established Rose. Your family home is sold and you want to take the rose you got from your parents with you. Just one example of why you might need to dig up a rose that has been in the same location for a number of years. However, it's the middle of summer and the rose is flowering.

Keeping the welfare of the rose in mind and if time permits, apply liquid seaweed in the weeks leading up to the shifting process to strengthen the rose and potentially reduce transplant shock. Trim the rose so that you can manage digging around the bush with a sharp spade to cleanly sever the roots about 30cm (12in) away from the crown, gently lifting the bush with each penetration.

For a very large old rose, you will need to go wider of the crown so as not to puncture the understock as this will encourage suckering once the rose is replanted. Roses don't really like us tampering with them at the root-zone and their amazing survival mechanism becomes activated, which might result in suckers forming.

When the rose is finally out of the ground, take the opportunity to prune away all deadwood and some of the oldest canes, then trim all branches neatly.

Have a trough already filled with water and liquid seaweed solution added so that you can immediately dunk the entire root ball and leave it in this solution for a few hours, or up to 24 hours where practicable. Then pot the rose into high-quality potting mix, giving it another good soak with liquid seaweed solution.

Should the rose need to be transported to another site for planting back into the soil, cover the roots with hessian or newspaper, which has been soaked in seaweed solution. This process will enormously reduce transplant shock and is vital to the success of relocating the rose. The roots must not dry out at any stage during transplanting.

Really large old roses are better removed using a backhoe or similar equipment that can lift the rose with roots intact. Once the rose is out of the ground you should remove some of the soil by tapping it away from the roots so that you can more easily access them to cleanly cut them. This will ultimately incur less damage to the root zone, which substantially reduces the likelihood of suckers forming.

3.23 Mulch the Rose Garden

Here are 30 reasons for using mulch in your rose garden:

- Improves soil conditions: binding sands and opening up clay
- Conserves soil moisture – mulch can save 73 per cent of what might be lost through evaporation
- Improves soil drainage
- Keeps soil temperatures cool during the day and warm at night
- Protects plants from frost damage
- Stops erosion
- Allows the soil to be worked earlier in the spring
- Saves time in cultivating and hoeing
- Prevents surface crusting, allowing the soil to breathe
- Reduces soil compaction
- Holds down weeds
- Prevents hardpans being created in the earth
- Provides nutrients, gases and other growth substances
- Prevents vitamin loss in plants
- Encourages nutrients to be taken up by the roots
- Improves the yield of crops
- Stops nutrients from being leached from the soil
- Hinders pests laying their eggs near to the plant roots
- Deters insects by its odour
- Reduces losses caused by soil-borne diseases

- Encourages earthworms and other micro-organisms
- Causes feeder roots to develop near the soil surface
- Encourages roots to penetrate deeper in search of food
- Stops plants wilting
- Shades seedlings from sunlight
- Makes plants more sturdy
- Improves the flavour and keeping quality of the harvest
- Protects the produce from mud-splash
- Recycles waste
- Improves the 'look' of the garden

So, there you have it, mulch is much, much more than just about saving water. A fantastic weed suppressant, mulch is the key to a low-maintenance garden. The correct selection of mulch can also increase the level of nutrients in the soil so mulching weeds and feeds plants in the one operation.

Mulch is simple to apply. Weed the garden bed, apply complete organic fertilizer over the soil, water and spread the mulch around, taking care to leave at least 10cm (4in) clearance around the base of the roses. Water well after application. For best results, top up the mulch layer at least once a year as it decomposes into the soil.

A simple rule is, the faster the mulch breaks down, the better it is for the soil, although if a long-term mulch is required, slower decomposition may be the preferred option. Scientifically, things break down according to the carbon to nitrogen ratio. The lower the carbon to nitrogen ratio, the faster the materials are broken down and the nutrients released into the soil. These levels can be estimated by looking at the mulch. The denser the structure, generally the higher the carbon content, and the longer it takes to break down.

A Quick Guide to Common Mulches ...

There are many different types of mulch available. In order to determine the best mulch for your garden, you must consider what you want the mulch to achieve, for example, only weed reduction and water conservation, or also helping your plants to grow.

Some of the more common mulches are listed with a quick guide on which to choose and dependent, of course, on what mulch is available in your locality.

Organic mulches can be created from either living or dead material. They will generally decompose in the soil, and can provide valuable nutrition for the plants. They suppress weeds, act as an insulator to 'even out' soil temperature and conserve water.

All organic mulches conserve water by reducing evaporation due to sun and wind, suppress weed growth, and encourage worm activity. Organic mulches hold and retain water for later use by the plants. Even the uneven surface of most mulch acts to prevent water run-off, helping water to be absorbed more readily into the soil.

Carbon/Nitrogen levels are noted in brackets. Note: the lower the first number, the faster the mulch decomposes and provides greater nutrients to the soil. The higher the first number, the longer lasting the mulch.

Lucerne (12/1) Lucerne (alfalfa) is the 'prince' of mulches, having a low carbon/nitrogen ratio. It is a mulch that breaks down quickly and adds substantial nitrogen and other beneficial elements to the soil. Lucerne breaks down to feed plants, stimulate biological activity and improve the soil structure.

Lucerne is an ideal mulch that feeds roses, it is also a compost activator. For best results buy lucerne which has been chopped into small pieces, otherwise the stalks can be very woody. As it decomposes quickly it will need topping up more regularly than other mulches.

If possible, know the source of the lucerne you purchase, because second- and third-cut lucerne will have fewer weeds than first-cut. This is especially important if the lucerne is organically grown and, ideally, has not been sprayed with weedicide.

Animal manure (12-20/1) All animal manures are great mulches. Fresh manure must be used cautiously as you can burn plant roots and it often contains weeds. Most animal manures can have a strong odour when fresh so consideration needs to be given to the wind direction from your garden to your home.

Any type of animal manure is best left to mature for a month or more prior to application on the garden. Manure is best added to the compost heap in layers, where it will break down to create humus that can then be used directly around the rose plants.

Since most animals are treated with worming inoculations, check with your manure supplier about when the animals were treated. What goes into the animal will definitely come out and the chemicals used might also kill the worms in your soil.

Composting first is the best way to make use of valuable animal manure.

Pea straw (25/1) Another nitrogen-rich material, pea straw breaks down quickly and conditions the soil and it is ideal around roses. Pea straw may contain a few pea seeds that will self-germinate. These can be easily weeded out or left to grow to provide natural nitrogen-fixing properties to the soil and edible peas to harvest for dinner.

Use a 'biscuit' of pea straw along the border of rose beds to reduce the incidence of birds flicking the pea straw off the garden and exposing the soil.

Seaweed (25/1) Ideal mulch with long-lasting properties. Seaweed is known to be beneficial in reducing pests and diseases but must be thoroughly washed to remove excess salt prior to lying directly onto the soil around roses. When using seaweed as a soil conditioner, add it in layers with manure in a compost heap to help it break down quickly.

Harvesting seaweed is illegal along some beaches so check with your local authorities prior to collection.

Leaf litter (60/1) Leaves provide excellent natural mulch, particularly if they have fallen from the trees within your garden. Autumn leaves can be distributed directly over any other mulch on the rose garden or added to the compost heap but they should never, ever be burned.

Sugar cane mulch (60–80/1) A good mulch but can be quite acidic so is best used only occasionally and in light layers around roses.

Wood chips/Pine bark (100–500/1) One of the most readily available mulches, wood chips are economical for large rose gardens where I recommend lucerne/pea straw immediately around the base of the roses and wood chips over the entire garden for an excellent long-lasting mulch to conserve moisture and reduce weeds.

Wood chips break down slowly and change colour as they weather.

Straw (Wheat or Barley) (80–100/1) Crop straw is high in carbon and takes longer to break down. In the rose garden, place this type of straw well away from the base of the roses because moisture sits in the straw and when that heats up it can cause sunburn on the rose stems.

We prefer to use this straw in biscuits along the border of the rose garden because it is heavier and birds cannot flick it away as easily. Placing damp newspaper underneath inhibits weed infestation of the rose garden.

Place biscuits of straw around the garden while tending the roses to reduce soil compaction. Use crop straw liberally on the compost heap to keep it warm and retain moisture within the heap.

Mushroom compost (31/1) A good-looking mulch material. However, it is not particularly nutritious, nor is it cheap to purchase. Care needs to be exercised with the pH level, as it is frequently too high (alkaline) which will restrict plant growth and cause leaves to curl. Definitely NOT recommended for use on a rose garden.

Sawdust (500/1) Makes a good mulch and reduces weed activity. It does not absorb moisture if applied too thickly. If used as a soil conditioner, apply some nitrogen fertilizer as it uses the nitrogen in the soil as it rots. Use sparingly on large areas between roses but not directly around the base of roses.

Course sawdust is ideal for weed-free pathways at the edge of the rose garden.

Newspaper (170/1) Newspapers 4–5mm thick provide good weed suppression and moisture retention when placed under mulch material. When using around roses, ensure that the newspaper is 10cm (4in) clear of the rose understock stem to allow moisture to penetrate under the layer of newspaper.

Non-organic Mulches These mulches may be man-made materials such as plastic, or mineral substances such as gravel. They are generally water-saving and help to even out the soil temperature. However, they do not provide any nutrients for the soil and can even starve plant roots of oxygen.

Gravel, scoria or pebbles are not recommended to use if you want to dig into the rose garden bed. Whilst conserving soil moisture and keeping ground temperatures even, weeds often become a considerable nuisance even where weed-suppressing mat is used beneath the stones.

Plastic might be excellent for keeping weeds at bay, however, it will encourage shallow root systems, stifles oxygen intake and definitely fails to add nutrients to the soil so is NOT recommended for rose garden beds.

Tips
- *Mulch is absolutely necessary in a rose garden.*
- *Don't apply mulch on windy days to avoid inhaling dust particles.*
- *Mulch encourages earthworms and microbes in the soil.*
- *Mulch retains soil moisture, maintains even temperature and inhibits weeds.*

3.24 Weeds around the Roses

Sometimes the only way to successfully stop invasive, creeping weeds in and around a rose is to dig up the entire plant, totally eradicate the invasive weeds then replant the rose. While you have the rose up out of the ground prune the roots, really clean up the rose bush by removing any dead wood and do a thorough winter prune. Soak the rose in a bucket with weak seaweed solution before you replant.

NEVER USE GLYPHOSATE HERBICIDE NEAR ROSES because it is a definite recipe for disaster. Roses will tolerate a broad range of difficult situations but they will not ever grow well once they have had a dose of glyphosate. The drift from these products can carry on a breeze and affect roses that are planted more than 100m (330ft) away.

The effect of glyphosate spray on roses will be evident about 5–7 days after spraying when all existing growth will dry up and turn brown. New growth will have very distorted foliage.

If you hire people to come and work in your garden, be diligent and ensure they never use glyphosate or spray your roses with equipment that has been used for weedicide or other chemicals.

Purchase two spray units, one for the rose spray maintenance program and the other one for all other chemical spray applications. Paint markers on both units so that you never get them mixed up yourself.

I could write an entire book about the disaster stories we have heard about roses and

Above: Mulched garden bed

herbicides; some of the stories are very funny, however most are quite sad because the end result is always the same – dead roses.

There are some very nearly dead husbands still walking around because we counselled their wives into forgiving them for spraying herbicide around the rose garden. We convinced the wife to see the happy, positive side of the situation – she could now plant new roses to re-invent the garden while the husband paid the bill as a reminder not ever to spray near her rose garden again.

The very best weed inhibitor is to keep a good thick layer of mulch around the roses throughout the whole year and top it up regularly. Ideally, keep the mulch about 10cm (4in) away from the base of the rose to allow new water-shoots to develop unhindered. The birds might keep flicking the mulch right up around the base but see this as another opportunity to NEED to be in the garden.

Hand weeding is a good physical task which can be a real pleasure – get down close amongst the roses and always remove weeds while they are small rather than let them settle in, become well established and potentially re-seed to cause an even greater problem.

Tips
- *Never use glyphosate near a rose garden.*
- *Maintain a thick layer of mulch around roses all year.*
- *Remove weeds when they are small to hinder re-seeding.*
- *Use weeding as your excuse to get up close and personal with the roses.*

3.25 Suckering Understock on Roses

This happens frequently when a rose is threatened during protracted periods of drought or where the roses are stressed, such as when they get too much water or not enough water. It is also prevalent if they are not firmly planted so they start to rock back and forth.

Sometimes it's grower error, which means that the understock was not 'eyed' properly at the very base and the grower at harvest did not detect this. The rose nursery retailer usually sees the problem at potting and either removes the 'eye' or discards the plant.

If you just trim the suckering understock at ground level, I assure you that within a short time, you will only have insignificant dark crimson blooms or clusters of tiny, single white blooms in spring and the budded rose variety will be gone. I urge you not to let that happen, but rather take action immediately when you first see the suckering understock while it is still immature or it will continue to grow wildly and eventually become a huge plant with a massive root-ball, making it very difficult to dig up manually.

To remove the suckers, get down on your hands and knees at the base of the plant, scrape back some soil near the sucker and see where it's growing from. Usually it will be attached to the understock and might be way down deep or could be quite obvious close to the surface.

Put your garden gloves on. Once you've revealed the source of the understock branch, grab hold of it and yank it really hard and fast – I liken it to when the kids had a loose tooth and I would ask them if I could take a look and wobble it maybe. Quick yank, tooth gone and kid wondering what the heck happened but excited about the tooth fairy coming that night.

When you've yanked the sucker away from the understock it is very important to check if there is a nice rounded end on what you pulled away. If you can see an 'eye,' which could be compared to a corn on your toe, then you have been successful in removing the sucker.

If not, get a sharp knife and remove the 'eye' by cutting inwards and upwards under the eye and inwards and downwards from above the eye.

Push the soil back over the wound and

Above: Sucker on a standard rose

give the plant a good dose of liquid seaweed to relieve any stress.

If the understock continues to grow after you have performed the above removal procedure, you may have to remove the entire plant and put a new rose in this location, but definitely have a go at removal first.

Should you not wish to bother removing the understock and would rather just plant a new rose in this location, dig very wide and deep to remove the rose as well as all the roots. Take a large barrow-load of soil away to be sure you've got all the understock roots out, then backfill the hole with fresh soil which is blended with compost from another part of your garden to reinvigorate the soil.

In this situation, I highly recommend waiting a few months before proceeding with planting a new rose just in case some of the understock roots re-activate. Rose understock is extremely tough and hard to kill – even with glyphosate weedicide, which I don't ever recommend.

Tips
- *Rose understock is very vigorous and very hard to kill.*
- *Roses are budded to understock to ensure their longevity.*
- *Remove suckers as soon as you see them.*

3.26 Pruning Roses

Pruning roses seems to be perceived as one of the most daunting tasks in the rose garden when really it doesn't need to be. Get a good pair of gloves, a clean and sharp pair of secateurs and just cut them – whichever way you do it, snip, snip or hack, hack, the roses will forgive you until you learn how to manage the task with more knowledge and confidence.

Attend a rose pruning demonstration at your specialist rose nursery or local garden centre where, seasonally, rosarians from the Rose Society in your area will be on hand to conduct pruning demonstrations and advice sessions to promote successful rose growing.

The more you prune your roses, the more confident you become and you will enjoy the rewards of pruning and grooming frequently. The quicker you remove spent blooms, the quicker new rose blooms have space and energy to grow.

As a general rule of thumb, prune back two-thirds of bush roses in winter and once they start to flower in spring, continually pick long stems of flowers for a vase to achieve the summer pruning requirement of pruning one-third of the bush overall.

All classes of roses are pruned using slightly different methods and climbing roses seem to cause the greatest consternation for rose gardeners.

Above: Pruning saw and sheath

Climbing roses require you to 'be the boss'. By pruning and maintaining climbing roses to grow as, how and where you want them is the key to creating a magnificent, well-established climbing rose.

Climbing roses should never, ever be cut right down to the size they were when first planted unless the growth was needed to be reduced prior to transplanting or possibly for renovation of the structure the climbing rose is growing on.

Tie down large canes and just trim the spent flowers from along the lateral canes leaving vertical, upright small branches on the main stem where new growth will emerge (see diagram).

A well-established four-year-old climbing rose growing in perfect conditions might have ten or more thick canes growing from the crown. To reinvigorate the climber and encourage new water shoot development you could completely remove two or three of the oldest canes from right down at the crown every year.

This pruning can be carried out during any season and will keep the climbing rose growing neatly within the allocated space. New water shoots will replace the woody old canes and give the climbing rose a fresh new look.

If a climbing rose is covering a structure it may never need to be pruned or you might get the hedge-trimmer and shear back all the twiggy growth along with the spent flowers as this will encourage fresh new foliage and another spectacular flush of flowering. There is no specific timing for this type of grooming a climbing rose.

Rambling roses which are typically only spring flowering should be cut back in early summer leaving some branches unpruned to be able to enjoy a spectacular display of

Above: Devoniensis climbing rose

rose hips in autumn. Immediately the hips are finished, prune the rest of the canes so they have time to set clusters of flowers for the next flowering season.

Modern shrubs, Floribundas and ground-covering roses can all be mechanically pruned using a hedge-trimmer, chainsaw or even running the lawnmower over them without affecting their ability to reproduce fresh, glossy foliage and another mass of blooms within less than 40 days during the flowering season.

These roses can also be groomed as neatly as you would a Hybrid Tea if you prefer a more gentle approach, but whichever way you prune them, the shrubs will ALWAYS produce a continual and prolific show of blooms.

You can have complete control over and maintain the size of many of the modern shrubs, Floribundas and ground-covering roses as most of them will continue to grow to a massive size if they're never pruned, yet they can be contained to neat-sized shrubs when groomed continually.

Prune modern shrub roses during any season in a temperate climate and they'll produce new growth and flowers almost continually throughout the year.

Hybrid Tea bush roses have a structure which requires more detailed pruning to maintain the shape of the bush and consistent repeat flowering. Pruning 25–30cm (10–12in) stems to an outward-facing bud encourages growth away from the centre of the bush, allowing good air circulation to reduce the incidence of fungal disease.

Above: Hybrid Tea Rose, Kardinal

Opening the centre of the bush in this way encourages development of long, strong stems, which are suitable to use for cut flowers in the vase.

Miniature roses can be pruned with hedge-clippers to almost ground level after each flowering and they will keep producing more and more flowers. At least once in each season remove all the deadwood at the crown to make way for fresh water shoots and to keep the bush neat.

Weeping roses should be left to establish long flowering canes out over the support ring for two or three years with just a light trim of spent blooms after each flowering. If you like the shape and size of the weeping rose, maintain it with light pruning. However, when it is extending growth beyond the space you expected, prune three or four canes from the crown of the weeper to reduce its spread. This can be done at any time but is definitely easier when there is little or no foliage during winter.

Despite having described the various pruning methods for the different classes of roses, they are very forgiving and will tolerate a fair amount of abuse when it comes to pruning.

Left: Our Rosy Red Carpet weeping rose   *Right: Summer's Evening weeping rose*

However, if you are unable to prune your roses yourself, supervise the pruning because an unqualified person can do a lot of damage by pruning roses which shouldn't be pruned or destroying the structure of roses which you've achieved by years of careful pruning and grooming.

I have heard some dreadful stories, such as where a glorious old-fashioned rambling rose was unnecessarily pruned to ground level and then took many years to recover and re-establish over an old barn. Lots of the old-fashioned roses, like *Rugosa* roses and their hybrids, should never be heavily pruned or they will perish.

A lady once told me she left a 'gardener' unsupervised to do her rose pruning and he actually dug up the roses, pruned them while up out of the ground and then replanted them. Most of those roses subsequently perished.

The reason they didn't like this treatment and died is that once pruned, the roses were planted directly back into the exact location where they had been growing for more than ten years. If the soil been removed or rejuvenated before the roses were replanted it might have been a success. Still, it was an unnecessarily complicated way of pruning roses (see also the section on transplanting a rose).

Rules for Pruning Roses
- Always wear protective clothing which gives you greater confidence and protects you from the prickles
- Use clean, sharp secateurs or mechanical equipment
- Remove all deadwood from right down at the crown of the bush
- Prune one-third in summer, two-thirds in winter
- Supervise the pruning if you cannot do it yourself

Tips
- *Pruning time is an opportunity to tidy up the rose garden.*
- *Clean and sharpen tools regularly whilst pruning.*
- *Wear protective clothing for confidence.*
- *Enjoy the results.*

3.27 Tools for use in the Rose Garden

Pruning Tools

Around the potted roses in the nursery my most-used tool is, of course, my secateurs, and I maintain them by keeping them always cleaned and sharpened. They've got my name on them and I prefer it if nobody else uses them. Not such a silly idea because, believe me, nobody will ever look after your precious tools the way you do.

Three years ago I developed calluses on the middle finger of my right hand, which I took as a sign that the bypass secateurs I had been using for more than 25 years were no longer suitable for me to use. My secateurs were always very well maintained and I regularly had them professionally sharpened. I think they were too heavy, although I suppose after 30 years of pruning roses my hands were starting to show the signs of that!

I started using a pair of anvil-cut secateurs, which is very lightweight and fits snugly in my hand. Maintenance is simple because both sides of the blade need three or four strokes with the sharpener; they're cleaned with non-chemical household cleaner and on occasion I spray the blade with olive oil.

When I get really serious about pruning, out comes my 'diamond'. The battery-operated Pellenc secateurs and hedger massively reduce the physical impact of pruning a large rose garden. I call this fabulous pruning gear my 'diamond' because to celebrate the occasion of our 25th wedding anniversary, being the practical rose gardener that I am I chose secateurs and a hedger rather than a diamond ring.

Loppers are very handy for removing thick canes on tall bushes, spent blooms on climbing roses and also for removing any deadwood and old branches from level with the crown at the base of a rose. The by-pass lopper is particularly handy for this job because the nose fits more easily between the thorny canes. Use the anvil-cut lopper to weight-reduce all the upper branches to make the pruning job easier.

Hedge trimmers are very useful for pruning shrub roses, ground-covering roses and miniature roses. Keep the manual hedge-trimmer well sharpened to reduce the physical impact on your shoulders and upper arms.

An electric/battery-operated hedge trimmer is appropriate to use on some of the climbing roses that produce massive clusters of flowers. Removing the spent flowers on modern shrub roses, floribundas, ground-covering and miniature roses immediately after flowering is a breeze with this type of hedge trimmer.

The lawn mower, set high with blades sharpened, will run over the ground-covering roses or other small shrub roses on the border of the garden bed and actually do a really neat job. The re-growth will be amazing.

Warning: it's best if you don't look at the roses for a few weeks after this type of pruning. I guarantee you, they will start to shoot again almost immediately and they will definitely flower again. These tough, hardy roses will also look more aesthetically pleasing because they'll be tidy compact shrubs rather than growing all sparse and spindly.

Above: Bucket of David Austin roses

Rules for Managing Pruning Equipment

- Maintain all your pruning equipment by regularly cleaning with gentle household soap. Bleach or any harsh chemical cleaners are definitely not necessary for cleaning secateurs. Rose virus can only be transferred by taking plant material from one rose to another through budding, and definitely not through pruning.
- Sharpened secateurs are very ergonomically pleasing to use and they don't damage the rose by bruising the stem, which can cause die-back. When I'm constantly pruning, I carry a small sharpener in my pocket and regularly stop pruning to sharpen the secateurs. This simple task makes my job so much easier.
- Wear a clip-on secateurs pouch so that you make a habit of ALWAYS putting your secateurs into a pouch to avoid leaving them lying in the garden for the mower to drive over them or throwing them, along with the prunings, onto the compost heap or, even worse, in the garden waste bin.
- Keep all your pruning and gardening equipment covered and out of the weather, so that every time you need it you can be confident it's clean, sharp, ready to use and will

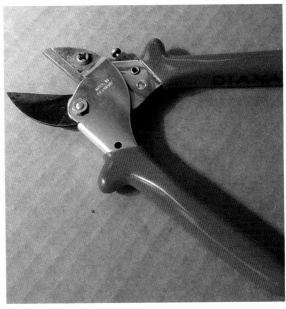

Left: Pellenc - Battery Shears   *Right: Anvil Cut Secateurs*

do the job at hand with ease.

- Buy only high-quality gardening equipment. Graham still uses a pair of secateurs that he inherited from his Dad and they must be more than 50 years old. That is quality because, when cleaned and sharpened, those secateurs are as good to use as when his Dad used them for the very first time.

My Favourite Garden Tool

In my repertoire of garden tools, my four-flat-tined fork is the handiest piece of equipment so I keep one undercover at both ends of the garden. I started using it exclusively when I realised I could dig planting holes without slicing through the worms as it distressed me to see half worms slithering about all over the place when I used the shovel.

A flat-tined fork digs the best planting holes because it doesn't cut a solid wall into the soil. It loosens the soil more readily so you don't have to lift heavy shovels full of soil out of the planting hole.

My fork lifts a comfortable amount of woody mulch, damp compost or animal manure and just about anything I need to shift around the rose garden. When using a shovel, I

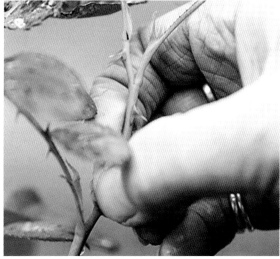

Left: Blind shoot   *Right: Finger pruning*

always want to fill it and stack it up which means that it becomes too heavy and stresses my body so that I tire more easily and what should be a pleasant task very soon becomes an exhausting one.

Tips
- *Only buy high-quality gardening equipment.*
- *Clean and sharpen secateurs regularly.*
- *Store tools out of the weather.*
- *Wear a secateurs pouch.*

3.28 Watering the Rose Garden

Roses LOVE consistent watering during the flowering season but HATE wet feet at all times.

A wet concrete path is not an accurate gauge to ensure your roses are adequately watered after a shower of rain. A rain gauge should indicate at least 6mm (¼in) of rain in one event before you decide not to water the rose garden or pots.

Even with heavily mulched garden beds, the roses need deep soaking of no less than 10 litres (21 pints) of water per bush, per week while they are establishing. Once the weather warms up and the roses are flowering, 20 litres (42 pints) per rose per week delivered in one soaking so that the water reaches right down to the root zone, will guarantee constant production of blooms and lush healthy foliage.

These quantities are a guide only for those gardeners who have well-drained, friable quality garden soil. Sandy beach soil may require double the quantity, whereas halving the quantity on well-mulched, heavy clay soil might suffice.

Before you set up a rose garden and start planting roses in your soil, it is vitally important to know about the type of soil you have and the watering requirements relative to your water pressure and flow rate. This is where I strongly advise consultation with your local professional irrigation specialist.

Every one of the different types of watering systems has been tried in our rose gardens during the past 30 years. Only now can I confidently say that our rose garden is very well irrigated because we have a professionally installed shrubbler system which is very water-wise efficient, economical and extremely low-maintenance.

I know the roses are happy because they continually produce masses of flowers and their foliage is always healthy due to not being subjected to overhead water from sprinklers. It's lovely to actually see water flowing out of the shrubblers when I'm on a maintenance round to check the system.

Should you still wish to proceed with installing a watering system yourself, here are some clues obtained from years of frustrating experience.

Do a simple test which will give you a reasonably accurate gauge of your flow rate and you can then be confident about which watering system might be most suitable for your garden. In order to do this get a 10-litre (21-pint) bucket, turn the tap on full pressure and fill the bucket. Accurately time how long it takes to fill the bucket. If it takes 10 seconds to fill, your flow rate is 1 litre (2 pints) per second or 60 litres (125 pints) per minute, which is about average in a suburban area with mains water supply.

Hose watering

Watering the garden with a hand-held hose or sprinkler is fine if you only have a small garden. The roses must be watered on a regular basis for them to perform to their maximum capacity. Leaving them to dry out for weeks on end and then watering every day will cause chaos for the plants and you will start to see incidence of disease and a decreased number of flowers.

Also, giving the roses a light squirt whilst walking around the garden enjoying the splendid evening fragrance with a beverage in one hand and a hose in the other is a definite NO-NO for your roses. The foliage will remain wet during the night and most certainly lead to the onset of fungal problems like blackspot and powdery mildew.

On the other hand, offering a regular good soaking whilst walking around first thing in the morning with a cuppa in one hand and a hose in the other is a great idea because the foliage will adequately dry during the day and you will have had the blissful experience of a morning in the rose garden.

Sprinklers should be used in the morning only and they can be a water-wasting hazard because it's so easy to forget to turn the tap off. A simple timer should be attached at the tap and used every time you turn on a manual sprinkler.

Recycled rubber soaker hose

This hose consistently delivers a slow and steady flow of water along the entire length of hose, is easy to install, very economical and environmentally friendly as it is made from 65 per cent recycled tyres.

The system should ideally be linked to a timer on the tap so that you cannot waste water by leaving a tap running. There are many models of timers available from dial control to mini-computer controls which can be adapted to add a soil moisture sensor in order to control water delivery.

Quantity of water delivery can be gauged by leaving a low dish under the soaker hose while the tap is on full pressure. After 5–10 minutes measure the quantity of water in the dish and this will give an indication of how long to set the timer for.

There must be a release valve inserted at the end of the line so that the lines can be flushed regularly. This is particularly important if gravity-fed dam water is used because clay particles may build up and block the line.

Where there are long narrow garden beds, the recycled rubber soaker hose is ideal, as you need just one length of hose along the centre of the bed to adequately water all the plants.

If you have a lot of different plants spread throughout a wide garden bed, loop the hose up and down in an 'S' shape, diagonally across the bed at 45cm (18in)

Above: Soaker hose

spacing to ensure thorough water output for all the plants.

The soaker hose should be pegged to the ground in direct contact with the soil, below the mulch.

Automatic watering system

Installing an automatic watering system in a large rose garden is the most practical, efficient, effective and economical (in both time and money) way to guarantee your roses get regular and adequate water which is exactly what they love.

A fully automated system will function from a set of solenoids wired to an easy-to-program yet sophisticated control panel with battery back-up in case of power failure. Soil moisture sensors should also be attached to turn the system off when it has rained or during seasons when the soil is adequately moist.

In-line drippers or shrubblers are more suitable for rose garden application because water goes directly onto the soil at the base of the rose and deep into the root zone of the plant, never on the foliage.

Above: Shrubbler on automatic watering system   *Above: Knockout*

In-line drippers

The water volume delivered to the roses is controlled by drippers inserted every 30cm (12in) on the inside of the pipe and water is slowly delivered to a concentrated area. Most dripper lines will deliver 1.5–2.5 litres (3–5 pints) per dripper per hour. The dripper capacity will need to be determined to adjust the length of time this system runs.

An in-line dripper hose is installed in parallel runs spaced 45cm (18in) apart, pegged directly on the soil and mulched over. This system is particularly efficient in sloped garden beds because of the slow water output.

Shrubblers are highly recommended for use in a rose garden as they offer more flexibility with adjustable flow rates and distribute the water over a wider area. When fully opened, delivery might be 40 litres (85 pints) per hour but the shrubbler head can be manually adjusted to half-open to deliver only 20 litres (42 pints) per hour. This

Above: Roses are water-wise plants

system is particularly efficient where lots of different types of plants with different water requirements are planted in the same garden bed, as is often the case in a rose garden.

Micro-sprays are not recommended in a rose garden because in windy conditions the water blows all over the leaves, which stay wet thus increasing the likelihood of fungal disease. There is also no guarantee that the water is deeply penetrating the root zone of the roses where it is most needed.

Here are a few points to consider when deciding which system might suit your requirements:

- You can easily install these irrigation systems yourself, however I recommend an irrigation professional for the installation of the fully automated system where solenoids and control panels require electrical wiring.
- All the above systems rely on mains water pressure. There are different systems used for a gravity-fed water supply.
- Once installed, all the different methods of irrigation can be added to or reduced as the garden establishes.
- If you rely on dam or bore water it is imperative to have regular water samples to test water quality for mineral/salt content. This water should never be sprayed over foliage unless used in a cocktail with fresh water.
- Where you may need to water the rose garden with water which has high readings of mineral/salt content, regular applications of seaweed solution will help to dissipate the salts in order to maintain health and vigour in your rose garden.

Tips
- *Roses are water-wise plants requiring minimum of 10 litres (21 pints) per rose per week.*
- *Never water roses late in the day.*
- *Research which is the best watering system to suit your garden.*

Next spread: City of Newcastle

Part 4: Healthy Roses organically, naturally

4.29 Healthy Roses – Eco-friendly, naturally

For the first couple of years of growing roses commercially, we used a plethora of chemicals because we thought that was the only way you could grow lovely roses and the chemicals were very readily available for us to buy and use.

We became disenchanted as more and more chemicals were recommended as one or other insect became immune to them and we were on a merry-go-round of spraying yet our roses always had blackspot and pests were a huge issue. The smell in the cupboard where those chemicals were stored was horrendous.

Graham did all the spraying back then and he could almost never wait to strip his clothes and shower immediately after doing a spray program. He started to talk about headaches and odd feelings after he'd been spraying. For ourselves, our children and all the people who were coming and going into our nursery, we had to find a more environmentally sound way of growing roses.

Together with our agronomist, who shared our concerns, we started to intensely research an eco-friendly method for growing roses. In the early 1990s, he suggested we start using Organic Crop Protectants (OCP) Eco-oil insecticide combined with naturally processed liquid seaweed solution as part of our spray management program whilst ensuring that the nutrition of our roses was adequately balanced by using high-quality organic fertilizer.

It was a costly exercise to have a company come to remove and dispose of all the chemicals we had been using but we knew they were not appropriate to place in our kerb-side garbage collection.

We've never looked back, as since that time we have only used high-quality, organically-certified products to consistently produce beautiful, healthy roses just as Mother Nature intended – eco-friendly, organically, naturally. Along the way we shared our growing methods with many gardeners and thankfully reduced the impact of harsh chemical use in rose gardens everywhere.

The aim with roses is to grow plants with high levels of vigour rather than trying to make them grow fast, and a complete organic humate fertilizer is used in conjunction with the rose maintenance spray program to achieve that.

Confidently use the range of eco-friendly products, eco-oil and eco-neem insecticides, eco-seaweed, eco-fungicide, and eco-aminogro (fish-based fertilizer) because when Mother Nature needs a gentle helping hand, this range of products offers just that.

Early in spring, before ladybirds are on the wing, aphids may need to be controlled so we add eco-neem to the spray program, often spraying more frequently until the ladybirds appear.

There must always be a few aphids and other insects and spiders in the rose garden because they are an indication that your garden is ecologically balanced and the ladybirds, along with other predators, will find a great source of nutritious food there. Your garden plays host to their breeding program and you should take a slow walk around the rose garden to see nature working.

Sometimes the weather creates environmental issues that affect healthy foliage and the roses can be afflicted by mildew and blackspot. We spray more frequently at the onset of humid weather.

Our recipe is simple, safe and economical:
To 10 litres (21 pints) of water, mix together ...
> ¼ cup of eco-fungicide powder
> ¼ cup of eco-oil (insecticide)
> Seaweed powder or liquid according to pack directions
> 20ml of eco-neem (insecticide) if necessary
> 50ml of eco-aminogro (plant and soil food)

Mix the ingredients well by having two or three buckets on hand to slosh the products backwards and forwards between the buckets before adding them to the spray unit or watering can. If you have a small spray unit, shake it vigorously before application.

Spray or pour over the foliage to run-off no less than once a month or more frequently at critical periods of the season or if pests and diseases are evident.

APPLICATION SHOULD ALWAYS BE CARRIED OUT PRIOR TO 10AM
NEVER SPRAY IF THE FORECAST TEMPERATURE IS OVER 30°C (86°F).

If you're passing the veggie garden or fruit trees on the way to the rose garden, stop and spray those too because there is always some opportunistic bug lurking around that area of the garden. The beauty of using these products to manage pests and disease on the edibles in your garden is that they are organically certified and there is no withholding period, so you can spray in the morning and harvest to eat in the evening.

We know that the healthier the plant, the greater its natural tolerance of and resistance to disease or pests.

Healthy, well-nourished roses will grow well without being forced and it is definitely possible to grow beautiful, healthy roses, which produce masses of glorious blooms without the use of harsh chemicals.

If a rose in your garden looks poorly and riddled with insects or defoliated by disease, this is what to do:

- Prune it by removing approximately half of all the branches
- Sprinkle a handful of organic fertilizer around the canopy of the bush
- Deep soak with no less than 20 litres (42 pints) of water
- Apply the rose maintenance spray to run-off
- Fluff-up the mulch or add 5cm (2in) layer of milled lucerne or pea straw
- Tell the rose you love it and walk away

Apply liquid seaweed weekly and within less than 45 days it will be flowering and you will be amazed at the complete transformation that a little bit of loving can create for a rose. Remember, from the words of the noted English rosarian, Rev. Dean Hole:

GIVE FOOD, WATER, AIR, SUN AND A LITTLE BIT OF LOVE
AND THE ROSE WILL REALLY REPAY YOU.
BUT, DENY THE ROSE WHAT IT DESERVES
AND YOU WILL GET THE ROSE THAT YOU DESERVE

Roses are so forgiving that if you don't put any effort or care into their performance, they might sulk and not flower while they aren't getting any attention. However, when you make time to love and care for them again, they will respond unhindered by giving you back every little bit of love and producing a mass of beautiful blooms once again.

About Eco-fungicide

Eco-fungicide sprayed over foliage affected by powdery mildew, blackspot and rust damages fungal cells resulting in rapid dehydration and the death of fungal growth. It also inhibits new fungal spores germinating by altering the pH on the foliage surface.

Eco-fungicide is completely harmless to beneficial insects such as bees and ladybirds. It is also safe for soil microbes, amphibians and earthworms when used around the base of rose plants.

About Eco-oil

Eco-oil is an organically certified insecticide made from a combination of natural plant oils (eucalyptus, melaleuca and canola) which penetrates the skin and blocks the breathing parts of sap-sucking and chewing insects like aphids, mites, scale, whitefly and caterpillars without harming beneficial insects such as ladybirds, hoverflies and lacewings. It is safe to use around bees.

Because Eco-oil contains no petroleum derivatives, only 100 per cent plant oils and extracts, there is reduced risk of foliage burn. However, it is best applied before 10am and only if the forecast temperature is below 30°C (86°F).

About Seaweed

Seaweed solution is a plant tonic which contains more than 60 vital nutrients, yet it is NOT a fertilizer.

As part of regular rose management, seaweed solution should be liberally applied over the leaves every 14 days because it contains a complex range of essential minerals, vitamins, amino acids and plant-growth regulators.

With regular application, seaweed solution will:

- Help the rose to produce up to 30 per cent more flowers
- Extend the vase life of rose blooms
- Offer 3–5°C (5–8°F) heat/cold tolerance during weather extremes
- Stimulate more vigorous root development
- Make the plant's immune system stronger for greater disease resistance
- Give higher quality flowers, fruit and vegetables
- Assist viable seed germination
- Reduce transplanting shock
- Act as a soil conditioner to unlock vital plant nutrients

Seaweed solution should be used in all aspects of garden care so that you will be successful – 'nothing beats success like success' especially in the garden!

About Eco-neem

Eco-neem is an organically certified insecticide made from an extract of the neem tree seed and combined with other plant oils. Once ingested by chewing and sucking insects, eco-neem supresses their appetite and distorts their growth cycle. It is not a knock-down insecticide as insects take a few days to die. During this time they stop feeding so no new damage occurs almost immediately after spray application. They are also weakened and are easy prey for other insects and larger predators like birds and lizards.

Eco-neem must be ingested for it to work, making it safe for 'good' insects that do not feed on plant foliage. There is no secondary poisoning so it's safe for a ladybird to eat an aphid that has ingested eco-neem.

About Eco-aminogro

Eco-aminogro is 100 per cent organic plant and soil food containing no additives and is manufactured using a unique process that aerobically digests solid marine wastes into potent bio-nutrient based liquid fertiliser. Natural enzymes and beneficial composting microbes are employed in the process to create a product full of highly plant-available nutrients, L-amino acids and vitamins.

Used as a foliage fertilizer, eco-aminogro will increase chlorophyll production and photosynthesis through the leaves and this increases the uptake of fertilizer that has been applied to the soil, resulting in a healthy, vibrant-looking plant.

Visit www.ecoorganicgarden.com.au for more information.

When your roses are not performing as you might expect them to, don't race off to the nearest department store to purchase an 'all-in-one rose spray gun' for what might seem a 'quick-fix' solution to the problem. Take a quiet moment to consider what environmentally friendly approach you could offer the roses to enhance their performance.

A little bit of loving and eco-friendly care goes a long, long way in your rose garden. It will also give you the enormous satisfaction of knowing that you are preserving our planet by allowing bees, frogs and many beneficial insects to get on with their business of working with us to create an environmentally safe place that we can all enjoy.

"A garden is a grand teacher. It teaches patience and careful watchfulness; it teaches industry and thrift; above all, it teaches entire trust" Gertrude Jekkyl

- *Tips for Spraying Roses*
- *Regular applications mean prevention rather than cure.*
- *Keep spray equipment clean.*
- *Never allow chemicals such as glyphosate to contaminate your spray equipment.*
- *Only make the quantity of spray required, as the spray cannot be stored.*

4.30 Rose Care

Roses are one of the easiest and most rewarding plants to grow when they are planted in well-drained soil in an open, sunny location in your garden. Watering, fertilizing and pruning will determine the robust health and flowering performance of your roses.

However, despite all your tender loving care and regular applications of our recommended rose spray maintenance program, there may be times when environmental factors create problems for your roses.

Fungal Disease

Blackspot is a fungus that occurs mainly on the lower leaves of the bush, evidenced by yellow leaves with black blotchy spots. Left untreated it can infest the whole bush and cause defoliation.

The disease becomes apparent after several hours of wet foliage during rainy periods or after heavy dew occurs. Stressed roses are more susceptible to blackspot.

I never get too concerned when I see a few spots on old foliage because the rose is constantly renewing itself and pushing all its energy into flowers and new growth.

Monthly applications of the rose spray maintenance program will assist in preventing blackspot fungus from invading the roses. Weekly application may be necessary during humid weather conditions.

Left: Blackspot fungus   *Right: Powdery Mildew*

Recently a friend of mine, in sheer exasperation, said: "Why is it possible to send a man to the moon and not stop blackspot? They should develop small 'rose fans' to blow along under the roses and keep the damp away". I have to admit I think it's a great idea, but who is going to invent them?

Downy mildew is a more insidious fungus than blackspot. It develops on new rose foliage and stems and is indicated by irregular brown blotches on the leaf surface and along the stems and can cause complete defoliation. Left untreated, downy mildew can kill roses. Newly forming blooms will not develop or open properly.

The disease only occurs in very moist, misty conditions and when the night temperature falls between 11–13°C (52–55°F). Downy mildew will not germinate when the temperature is above 18°C (64°F).

Keep a check on night-time temperature and humidity. Weekly applications of the rose spray maintenance program will inhibit the fungus from spreading.

Powdery Mildew is initially evident when the leaves curl and discolour to look almost purple. The rose maintenance program should be sprayed immediately before white powder appears or the fungus will spread rapidly and distort developing flower buds. Roses which are planted in shade or in filtered light near trees, under the eaves close to the house, in a glass house or in an air-less part of the garden will nearly always be afflicted by powdery mildew fungus and should be relocated to another part of your garden.

Some older rose varieties are very susceptible to powdery mildew at the slightest hint of inclement or humid weather. I call those roses 'mildew magnets' and suggest they be planted in the hottest, most windy part of the garden, or more usually I recommend selecting a healthier variety.

Interestingly, roses susceptible to powdery mildew are planted at the ends of grapevine rows so the vigneron knows when the roses show signs of powdery mildew, a spray program should be implemented to protect the grapevines against powdery mildew and other fungal diseases.

Botrytis fungus is usually evident on pale-coloured blooms immediately after rainy weather. Dark pink spots appear on the flower petals and there is no cure. Trim the affected blooms if you find them unsightly.

Rust is evident when spores of orange powder appear on the underside of the foliage after spells of damp and cool weather conditions where there is inadequate ventilation. Roses planted in very poorly drained soil are particularly vulnerable to rust fungus.

Apply the rose maintenance spray to the underside of the foliage if possible and consider relocating affected roses to a more open part of the garden or fork holes into soil around the roses to aerate the soil and improve drainage.

Insects and Other Pests

Aphids are those tiny sap-sucking insects which appear in early spring when all their predators are still sleeping off the winter. They invade the juicy, fresh young tips, which are loaded with nutrients and will always take advantage of roses that are planted in a more sheltered position in the garden.

Unfortunately, if not kept in check early they will distort the first long-anticipated rose blooms of the season. All the affected buds will soon be bent over and distorted so that the blooms will be small and will not open properly. Prune off affected stems to make way for new growth and more flowers as quickly as possible.

Above: The Children's Rose with botrytis

The rose maintenance spray program should be commenced in late winter after pruning or in early spring as soon as new foliage appears on the roses. This prevents aphids developing much beyond the larval stage and will interrupt their breeding cycle.

Aphids in small numbers are an indication that your garden is environmentally well balanced and will entice the ladybirds to emerge from their winter slumber knowing they have a good food-source while they are busy breeding.

Thrips

These pesky critters fly in on hot winds and leave a trail of destruction, mainly on pale-coloured blooms where their damage is very evident by brown markings on the petals. They are almost invisible to the naked eye as they burrow deep down into the petals of rose blooms, which makes them difficult to eradicate by spraying.

Left: Aphids   *Right: Thrip on Pierre de Ronsard*

When the infestation is significant they suck the immature flower bud, which prevents the bloom from opening.

Eco-neem oil can be added to the organic rose maintenance spray program to keep thrips controlled while hot winds are prevalent. However, we usually prefer to trim affected flowers because it is very difficult to get the spray deep into the flower buds where the thrips are hiding.

Whitefly

A modern pest that looks like a tiny moth is becoming more prevalent due to over-use of pesticides that have killed off its natural predators. Hordes of whitefly breed rapidly under rose foliage where they suck the sap and leave white lesions visible on the upper-side of the foliage.

The foliage loses vigour and is less able to photosynthesise so the entire growth system of the rose is compromised.

The organic rose maintenance spray program with added eco-neem oil must be sprayed under the foliage to interrupt the whiteflies' breeding cycle.

Red spider mite

Usually only found in very dry parts of the rose garden where there is minimal air circulation, the red spider mite hides under foliage where it creates an almost invisible web and breeds voraciously while sucking the foliage dry.

Spider mites hate water, so spraying under the leaves for a few days may minimise their numbers but the rose maintenance spray program with eco-neem oil added will definitely interrupt their breeding cycle.

Increase the level of moisture to this part of the garden to decrease the likelihood of red spider mite reinfestation.

Scale

Usually found on lower stems of rose plants, this sap-sucking insect, if left to prosper and spread upwards, can seriously weaken the host rose. Scale is often seen on stems of potted roses, which is a sure sign that the plant is root-bound in the pot; there is soil compaction and poor drainage.

Repot contained roses and scrape the scale from the stems. Thoroughly spray the plant, particularly the stems, using the organic rose maintenance spray and adding eco-neem oil for complete control.

Caterpillars

Not as attracted to roses as they are to the orchard or vegetable garden, I usually recommend that when you see a caterpillar, pick it off and dispose of it. To be on the safe side, it is a good idea to add eco-neem oil to the next organic rose management spray program to control the caterpillars while they are still at the larval stage.

Other insects

There may be an occasional swarm of insects like soldier beetles that decide your garden is worth a visit. There is no point spraying them because they'll be there for a short time, probably pollinating your roses without you knowing what's going on in your garden and then fly off because they filled their bellies at your place and will go and see what is on offer in another garden.

Damage from swarms of these insects is minimal with maybe some browning on the outer petals of rose blooms. See this as an opportunity to deadhead the spent flowers to make way for lovely fresh foliage and flowers.

Plagues of **grasshoppers** or **locusts** may appear to have done a lot of damage when you first see the bushes after they've ravaged your roses. They should leave an account for their summer pruning expertise because the roses will respond by producing the grandest autumn flowering you ever did see, especially if you go round and tidy up by trimming the stems after the grasshoppers and locusts munched them.

Earwigs and some **beetles** which live and breed in the mulch, leaf-and rose petal-litter at the base of the roses, need to walk up the stems of the roses to get into the flowers where they feed on pollen and sweet rose nectar.

If you have a particularly large outbreak of crawling insects, smear a thick layer of petroleum jelly around all the lower stems of the roses because the earwigs and beetles won't walk over it.

Encourage birds into the rose garden by regularly filling birdbaths with fresh water. The birds will return your favour by eating a host of various insects to keep numbers balanced and reduce any potential damage to the flowers.

Before you go to the supermarket and buy a spray gun of potentially lethal chemical to spray the roses whenever you see insects on them, think about why that insect is in your garden. It may well be there as a predator which has selected your garden to feast on the larval stage of a far more destructive insect.

It is definitely there for a purpose so identify the insect and research its habits and whether it is doing any real damage in the garden. You might consider leaving it for the birds to devour.

Know that Mother Nature, if left mostly to her own devices will manage all the insects in your garden. While it may rile you that sap-sucking aphids distorted a few of the early spring rose blooms that you were so longing to see open in all their glory, patience and observation will alert you to when and how you may need to step in and interfere with the natural processes in an eco-friendly garden.

Walk gently on the Earth and the rewards will be immense for your children and their children's children.

4.31 Season-by-season Rose Management

Winter

This might be considered the busiest month in a rose garden because it's pruning time. In temperate climates you can start pruning in the first weeks of winter. However, if you live in a very cold climate, wait until the last weeks to be sure the heavy frosts are over.

Winter is also the time to plant new bare-rooted roses which you pained over selecting from catalogues or saw flowering in other gardens throughout the previous months, placed on order and have been patiently waiting to receive in the post.

During winter the rose garden should also be consistently watered because, once pruned, the roses will immediately start actively growing. If you get good winter rain in your area, turn off the automatic watering system or check the soil moisture sensor is activated. Ensure that the roses get at least 10 litres (21 pints) (one bucket) of water per week.

Apply a fortnightly dose of seaweed solution and commence the organic rose maintenance spray program as soon as the pruning is completed.

Sprinkle a small amount of fertilizer around each pruned bush and cover the soil with a light application of straw mulch. Enjoy the fruits of your labour – a beautifully pruned, tidy-looking rose garden, which can now be left to produce fresh growth for bountiful spring flowering.

Spring

The season of anticipation; the rose garden is poised and ready to burst forth with flushes of beautiful blooms. Healthy new foliage can be host to aphids so be watchful and to keep them at bay continue monthly applications of the organic rose management spray because it may take the ladybirds a while to catch up with the aphids and they will damage the first flowers if left to go on a rampage on all the lush new growth.

Hopefully you will have planted lots of late winter and early spring flowering bulbs and other plants because all the flowers and warm sunny days will encourage ladybirds to start their breeding and they will be active in good numbers while feasting on aphids.

These are all the signs of a healthy eco-friendly garden, so if you see a few aphids on the new buds, don't panic and squash them because very soon, you will also see ladybirds and other predators. Your rose garden is ecologically balanced when you see balanced numbers of all types of insects.

Where no harsh chemical sprays are used to destroy the aphids and their predators, small birds like wrens, sparrows and pardalotes will happily become a very handy, delightful addition to your rose garden and their twittering with each other heralding another branch of scrumptious aphids is to be right there witnessing Mother Nature at her supreme best.

Finger prune around 15–20cm (6–8in) off one-third of the tips on each bush. This very simple task will lessen the number of flowers in the first flush but at the same time, it will strengthen the plant to encourage deeper root penetration. This will, in turn, create strong basal shoots (water shoots) and guarantee continual and prolific flowering on well-established, sturdy bushes throughout the season.

Trim off or finger prune any blind shoots because they are unproductive and will never flower. They will also waste valuable energy by delaying the production of healthy flowering stems.

Blind shoots occur especially during spring because warm sunny days promote lots of sugar and carbohydrate-filled sap to flow through the lush new growth. If there is a very cold or frosty night, the sap is hindered from moving freely throughout the plant system and is stalled at the most cold point, the tip. This creates a blind shoot.

Whenever there are warm sunny days, your roses are producing new growth and if there is a spell of cold nights, carefully observe the growing tips. Once you recognise the difference between a blind shoot and a healthy flowering stem, trimming or finger-pruning them becomes a natural thing to do.

The sooner all blind shoots are removed from the bush, the sooner the rose can push all its energy into strong flowering stems.

Now is the time to feed the soil with quality complete organic fertilizer sprinkled around the canopy of each bush and continue feeding every eight weeks during the entire flowering season. Pour liquid seaweed solution over the foliage at least once a month to strengthen and maintain healthy foliage.

Start picking flowers for vases inside your home.

Summer

Water, water, water = blooms, blooms, blooms. Check that all the drippers on the watering system are functioning and set the automatic timer to deliver approximately 20 litres (42 pints) of water per watering interval. During extremely hot weather extend this to twice weekly.

Spent rose blooms should be trimmed constantly; removing about 30cm (12in) of stem will ensure strong new regrowth. This also keeps the bushes neat and tidy rather than spindly and leggy. As a general rule, one-third of the rose bush should be pruned throughout the summer and this can be carried out over a period of time to ensure that the rose always carries a good cover of foliage.

Leaves are the food factory of the rose and will maintain moisture and energy within the plant to ensure continual flowering while protecting the stems from sunburn. Enjoy vases of flowers in the house but never take every single stem from a rose bush during summer because when you cut flowering stems you are also removing the protective canopy of leaves that are keeping the plant cool.

Spent flower bracts on shrubs and ground-covering roses can be pruned with a hedger where the roses are irrigated and this will promote rapid regrowth of foliage cover to prevent sunburnt stems. These varieties are guaranteed to be re-flowering within 30–45 days.

Fertilize all the roses again during summer and regular applications of liquid seaweed solution will offer between 3–5°C (5–8°F) heat tolerance. Top-up the layer of mulch so that the soil is completely covered to gain maximum benefit from the irrigation and to keep weeds under control.

Periods of summer rain may cause humidity, which increases the likelihood of mildew and blackspot on the foliage. The organic spray management program should be carried out on days when the temperature is not expected to reach more than 30°C (86°F).

Autumn

This is the season for rose-loving gardeners! Glorious cooler days after a hot summer mean that autumn is the most anticipated season in the rose garden. Now is the time to plant the potted roses you collected and retained in pots during summer and to start preparing the rose garden for winter planting.

The true depth of colour in rose flowers becomes evident as the nights get cooler and the sun loses its summer intensity. Gather rose catalogues and visit rose gardens in your area. Take lots of photos and start compiling your wish-list of new roses to order for winter planting.

Continue with the rose maintenance spray program. Cool nights and damp air will increase the likelihood of fungus attack. Be watchful and if necessary increase the spray program to weekly applications as soon as the weather changes. Healthy, well-foliaged plants will provide masses of richly coloured blooms right up to winter pruning time.

During the last weeks of autumn, visit rose specialist nurseries and garden centres which often have end-of-season sales in order to disperse the potted roses which have been managed in pots for the last nine months. The roses will be very well established and bursting to be planted in your garden.

By planting roses during autumn, roses become nicely established prior to winter pruning and you will enjoy beautiful large bushes in their first flowering season in your garden.

Tips
- *Never toss fertilizer onto wet foliage.*
- *Prevention is better than cure – do monthly applications of organic spray maintenance program.*
- *Leaves are the food factories of rose bushes.*

4.32 Roses for Your Health

Growing roses for your health is not just about the vitamin C in the rose hips, which by the way contain bioflavonoids as well as vitamins E and D, essential fatty acids and antioxidant compounds. Rose hip extracts are found in syrups and those who suffer from rheumatoid arthritis, poor immunity, constipation, mild gallbladder disorders and kidney and bladder conditions often use creams. Let your garden be your doctor.

Growing roses is very much about the fact that your rose bushes NEED you to be with them out in the garden. They beg you to snip the spent blooms so that they can produce more flowers; there will be an odd weed or two to pull out, and some mulch to push back onto the garden that the birds scratched over the path.

When you see how well they respond to a little bit of tender loving care, you will need to fertilize the roses more frequently, apply the rose maintenance spray every month and pick flowers for vases inside more often.

Reciprocally, you NEED roses. Rose bushes won't just fill a space in the garden at your place. Their flowers are good for your soul; they incite a feeling of well-being, happiness and optimism. If you're cross at the world or somebody within your world, take the secateurs and start trimming spent rose blooms and I know from vast experience that you cannot and will not stay cross for very long.

Roses offer a sense of peace to console you if you're sad or hurting. They energise you when you're feeling down. A garden with even a few roses will force you out of the house to tend them where you'll have the sun on your face, the wind in your hair and the amazing satisfaction of a beautiful space to live in.

Because your place looks so lovely, other neighbours in the street will become inspired to take more pride in their garden and this will have a huge impact on the self-esteem of all age groups within your community.

There are many statistics about the health force of gardening that confirm how 'green space' has such a beneficial impact on our health and well-being.

Just 15 minutes spent in your garden each day will hugely assist your mental health status, improve your circulation and get you exercising without even knowing you're doing it; bending to pull a weed, stretching to reach a rose which needs to be trimmed from the bush right at the back of the garden bed, sweeping the path and even holding the hose to water the pots requires you to move around and interact with the life-force of your garden.

A garden which has beautiful, fragrant roses incorporated adds a whole other dimension to 'green space' and significantly alters the environment where you live because roses make people smile, they induce happiness and you'll live to a ripe old age because you just have to be out there looking after your roses.

4.33 *What is wrong with my Rose?*

Here are some of the most common reasons of what goes wrong and why ...

Potted rose not performing after planting in the ground

When you plant a new potted rose in your garden you may expect it to endure some transplanting shock. This can be reduced by soaking the newly planted rose with a liberal dose of seaweed solution at the rate of one 10-litre (21-pint) watering can per bush at planting. Leave it to settle in without any more attention for a couple of days and definitely DO NOT keep watering it.

If, after a week or so, the new rose still looks unhappy or the foliage is drooping and falling off, don't just leave it in the ground to suffer. Dig it up and pop it back into a pot, give it a light trim and soak it again with seaweed solution.

There is most definitely something wrong in the soil where you planted the rose and you may discover the reason when you dig it up. Here are a few things that might be wrong

- There is rotting compost or fertilizer at the base of the hole – the roots are severely compromised and will die so the new rose has no support system
- The hole is lined with clay and water is sitting in the hole like a sump – the rose is drowning
- The rose is not getting enough water – the soil may be hydrophobic (resisting water) and needs soil-wetter, compost and mulch

Bare-rooted rose not performing after planting

If you purchased your roses by mail order, open the parcel immediately to check the quality of your new rose plants and get them into a bucket of weak seaweed solution. They can remain soaking for up to 24 hours.

Should it not be possible to plant the roses immediately after soaking, they should be heeled into friable soil in the garden or quality potting mix in a large tub until time permits you to plant them into their allocated space. Soak them after heeling-in to dispel air from drying the roots.

The roots should NEVER dry out.

Most bare-rooted roses hit the ground and start to produce new shoots almost immediately and certainly should have new growth happening within two weeks of planting.

Some roses are a bit slower to get going and take longer to settle in. If they have not produced evidence of new growth after three weeks there is probably an issue with the soil. If you cannot diagnose the problem, take action immediately by digging up the roses and putting them in pots.

Check the following:
- If the soil is sopping wet, raise the soil profile and place a slotted drainage pipe to drain water away from the rose bed
- NO FERTILISER or anaerobic (non-decomposed) compost or other material should be under the roots – only seaweed solution should be used when planting new roses
- Severe frost would be indicated by blackened stems – replant closer to spring when frosts are over
- Crinkled dehydrated stems indicate the roots were left to dry out either prior to or after planting.

Once any issues with the soil are rectified and you are confident the soil is adequately conditioned for bare-rooted roses to grow happily, replant the roses. Dehydrated roses with crinkled stems should be thrown away because they will never recover.

Sunburn on roses

Roses will not die from the effects of sunburn. However, the lower branches on rose stems are very susceptible to sunburn when there is inadequate foliage to shade those branches and evaporated moisture in the thick stems is not replenished as quickly as in the upper-storey leaves during hot weather.

Sunburn can occur in early spring after frost when rose stems are still bare on newly planted roses or after pruning. The hot spring morning sun can penetrate frozen plant tissue and cause burning on vulnerable stems. Regular applications of liquid seaweed offers between 3–5°C of protection against frost damage so should be applied regularly after winter pruning and planting.

Wet mulch material, which is in contact with the lower branches, will heat up when exposed to hot sun and can cause sunburn on those branches. Keep all mulch materials away from the lower stems at the base of the roses.

Where lower branches of roses are facing very hot afternoon sun, plant low shrubs at the base to shade the rose with a canopy of leaves that will reduce vulnerability to sunburn.

At pruning time, the sunburned branches should be pruned allowing space for new water-shoot development.

Nutrient deficiencies evident on foliage

The health status of your roses is generally indicated in the colour of the leaves that are normally mid-dark green and in good proportion to the size of the plant.

Above: Moonbeam with Blue for You in background

Miniature roses have small foliage, modern shrubs produce glossy medium-sized foliage, while many hybrid teas and huge climbing roses have large leaves.

When you notice discolouration or distortion of leaves on roses in your garden there is usually a nutrient deficiency, which can be easily corrected by applying a spray of trace elements powder combined with seaweed solution. These should correct minor nutrient deficiencies and unlock stored fertilizer in the root zone.

If you see no change in the new foliage after this application, take leaf samples to your local specialist rose nursery or garden centre for further identification. Should a serious problem be diagnosed, take foliage samples for laboratory leaf analysis.

Whatever goes wrong

There are no absolutely hard and fast rules about growing roses. Follow your intuition and do whatever you think the rose needs at the time when you see it performing poorly. Your solution will usually send a message to the rose that you are caring and it may respond by producing a beautiful bunch of rose blooms. If that doesn't happen, dig it up and throw it away. Put humus-rich soil in that location and plant a healthy new rose.

Above: Cooper on his way to plant a rose

The Final Word

1. Buy only quality rose plants – quality is a two-year-old, vibrant and healthy looking rose on virus tested under stock with growing instructions and a guarantee.
2. Plant roses only in sunny positions with a minimum of 5 hours' sun per day – roses are guaranteed to flower profusely and maintain health and vigour in such a location.
3. Plant the roses into well-drained soil – clay is great, especially when blended with quality compost - the soil you have is always preferred to imported soil blends.
4. Feed your roses regularly – one half handful per plant every eight weeks with balanced complete organic fertiliser.
5. Roses love wind and good air circulation to maintain healthy, disease-resistant foliage. Companion planting with annuals, perennials and bulbs is encouraged but needs to be maintained.
6. Mulch with lucerne, pea straw or the pine bark products – mulch maintains soil moisture, increases worm and microbe production and reduces weeds.
7. We recommend the rose maintenance spray program at least once a month – seaweed solution mixed with eco-insecticide and eco-fungicide will increase strength in the foliage to combat pest and disease problems.
8. Deep soak rose plants with 20 litres (2 buckets) per bush twice a week to establish; a soaker system with timer will soak to the root zone and save water ... roses are very water wise and don't like wet feet.
9. Prune regularly, trim and groom as flowers finish. Summer prune by one third and winter prune by two thirds. Always use sharpened and clean secateurs and wear protective gloves for confidence and comfort.
10. Take time to smell, love and enjoy the roses in your garden!

Acknowledgements

There has been a book in me since I can remember. New Holland invited me to get it out of my head and onto paper; this is the result and I thank them for the opportunity to share my passion for roses with you.

The world didn't stop while I was writing this book but my family might have felt it did because I became so focussed and they took a 'back-seat' for the journey. Thanks to you all for your patience and understanding.

Some beautiful friendships blossomed while I was compiling this book. Carolyn was there from early morning to late night, coaching, counselling and caring; Jeanette sat in the sun amongst the roses, sketching; Virginia organised the photo shoots and became my 'hands-on assistant' with the book and in the rose nursery. My delightful niece, Katrina was the professional photographer (InVision Photography) who captured the true beauty of our rose garden.

Graham, the love of my life, the one who introduced me to a beautiful world of roses and with whom I have harmoniously shared this connection with Nature, thank you for your encouragement and support which afforded me the opportunity to write all we know about roses.

Special thanks to Olga, Simon and Caryanne at New Holland for seeing this beautiful book to fruition.

Last but not least, to the 'Queen of Flowers', the roses, I say thank you for teaching me so much and giving me such pleasure and joy in my life – not a day goes by, in all seasons, that I don't stop and wonder at your magnificent beauty.